Ernie PYLE
An American war correspondent in Normandy
summer 1944

Ernie PYLE
An American war correspondent in Normandy
summer 1944

Ernie Pyle with Generals Bradley and Eisenhower.
© *Indiana State Museum 68.991.008.0710*

Introduction

Ernie Pyle, apace with the troops[1]

On 18 April 1945, all America was bereaved: on the Island of Iejima, amidst the throes of the Battle of Okinawa, a Japanese soldier had just shot down Ernest Taylor Pyle, at the age of 44 years. That day, it was as if every American - including President Truman himself - had lost a close friend. For Ernest Taylor Pyle, more commonly known simply as Ernie Pyle, was considered to be the greatest American war correspondent of his time. He was believed to carry the very voice of those ordinary GIs, by all American families with a father, a son or a brother posted on one of the many battlefields where the U.S. Army was engaged.

Immersion, integration

Born in 1900 and the son of a farming family from Indiana, in Midwest America, Ernest Taylor Pyle was 23 when he completed his studies and started his first job as a journalist for the *La Porte Herald*, the local newspaper in La Porte, Indiana.

---

1. We would like to inform our readers that the dates indicated at the start of each article are the dates they were published in American newspapers. Consequently, they can be up to two weeks after the events they cover. Hence, the articles describing the progression of an infantry company in Cherbourg were published as of 12th July, whilst the town was, in fact, liberated on 26th June.
There are several reasons for this interval. First of all, the fact that Ernie Pyle did not necessarily write his papers out in the field - he waited to have a good, full story to do so. Then, once the papers written, they had to pass military censorship.
When finally approved, they could be sent to the newspapers for publication. Dates are written in U.S. format.

After a few months, he returned to the *Washington Daily News*, which was part of the Scripps-Howard media group, reuniting - at the time - several newspapers and radio stations across the United States and founder of the United Press agency. Ernest Pyle specialised in aviation. He then learned that total immersion in a subject was the best way to write good papers. He also discovered that he was capable of easily integrating a group and of telling its story in a simple manner to his readers.

In 1934, by now an experienced journalist, Ernest Pyle was appointed as special correspondent for the Scripps-Howard group. He chose his own subjects, writing what he wanted, when and where he wanted, provided that he delivered on average 6 columns of text per week to the group's newspapers and their claimed readership of 13 million. Up to 1940, he covered the continent 35 times, offering an in-depth insight into America and the Americans... to the Americans.

From Ernest to Ernie

In November 1940, Pyle set off on his very first foreign expedition. He left to 'cover' the Battle of Britain, telling the story of the struggle by the RAF pilots to counter the German aviation, the ruins of Coventry, and civilian life in London's shelters. Yet, this initial experience was not enough for Pyle, who felt like a 'tourist watching the war from his balcony.' What he really wanted was to live the war 'at ground level', huddled in foxholes along with the combatants.

So, from June 1942, he began to cover training of the first American troops to be sent to England. Then, in November 1942, he accompanied the same troops when they landed in North Africa. It was his own baptism by fire. It was also an opportunity to perfect his working method and his style, since he remained for several days, or even weeks, with a unit before withdrawing to write his articles. Ernest Pyle covered the war like the soldiers did: out in the field and in action. He observed, talked, and rarely took notes. And he wrote about how the soldiers lived, fought, idled, entertained, chatted, pondered, joked... and died. As he spoke of the ordinary Americans engaged in the army and the war, to the ordinary Americans back in the homeland, Ernest Pyle gradually became 'Ernie' Pyle, equally familiar with simple soldiers as he was with generals, but also with their families, who read the hundreds of newspapers owned by the Scripps group across the nation.

After North Africa, Pyle followed the American troops - the infantry units in particular, for whom he had developed an almost fraternal affection - in Sicily. In August 1943, he returned to the United States where he was welcomed like a star of the silver screen, giving a multitude of interviews, posing for a Chesterfield cigarette advertisement, answering letters and phone calls from soldiers' wives, and being intensely questioned by members of parliament on the morale of the boys on the other side of the Atlantic.

A Pulitzer Prize earned out in the field

Pyle became weary of such honours and social chitchat to which he failed to relate, and he set off for the Italian front in November 1943. Then, in the spring of 1944, he was back in London, to observe preparations for the Normandy Landings. It was at this point that he learned of his Pulitzer Prize, awarded to America's best journalists. So, it was as a highly experienced war correspondent, famed and even worshiped by some, who arrived in Normandy on the morning of 7 June

1944. An aura that failed to fluster Pyle, who did nothing to change his working habits and his writing: as close as possible to action, as close as possible to the troops, telling the story of the soldiers' day-to-day lives, simply and warmly.

Ernie Pyle stayed in France until late September 1944, hence covering the entire Battle of Normandy and the liberation of Paris. In three months, he wrote 70 articles, telling, not only the story of the Channel crossing, the capture of Cherbourg, the bombardments during Operation Cobra, but also the routine of the servers in an artillery battery, or the beauty of the Normandy landscapes. These 70 articles are reunited for the first time in this book.

'I would go off my nut.'

After the euphoria of the liberation of Paris, Ernie Pyle left Europe, exhausted by the war. 'All of a sudden it seemed to me that if I heard one more shot or saw one more dead man, I would go off my nut. And if I had to write one more column, I'd collapse. So, I'm on my way,' he explained to his readers in the first paper he wrote in France.

Back in the United States, Ernie Pyle was snatched up once more by the 'obligations' associated with his immense popularity. Among others, he signed a contract with Hollywood for a cinema adaptation of the articles he wrote in North Africa and Italy, *Here is Your War*. The filmmaker William Wellman then produced *The Story of GI Joe*, starring Robert Mitchum in one of the leading roles.

However, Ernie Pyle was never to see *The Story of GI Joe*. In January 1945, he set off once more for the Pacific, where he was killed on his way to start a new article.

Frédéric Patard

A genuine miracle

6/10/44
On the Normandy Beachhead

It will be several days before military security permits us to describe in much detail the landings just made in the long-awaited Allied invasion of Europe.

Indeed, it will be some time before we have a really clear picture of what has happened or what is happening at the moment. You must experience the terrible confusion of warfare and the frantic nightmarish thunder and smoke and bedlam of battle to realize this.

So, we will take up this short interval by telling you how things led up to the invasion from the correspondents' viewpoint. This column is being written on a ship in a convoy, crossing the English Channel, so that it will be ready to send back to England by dispatch boat as soon as we hit the beach.

When we secretly left London a few days ago, more than 450 American correspondents were gathered in Britain for this impending moment in history.

But only 28 of those 450 were to take part in what was termed the assault phase. I was one of those 28. Some of the rest will come over later, some will cover other angles, some will never come at all.

We assault correspondents were under military jurisdiction for the past month while waiting. We had complete freedom in London, but occasionally the Army would suddenly order us in batches to take trips around England.

Also, during those last few weeks we were called frequently for mass conferences and we were briefed by several commanding generals. We had completed all our field equipment, got our inoculations up to date, finished our official accrediting to Supreme Allied Headquarters, and even sent off our bedrolls 10 days before the final call. (We will rejoin them some time later on this side -we hope).

Of the 28 correspondents in the Assault Group about two thirds had already seen action in various war theaters. The old-timers sort of gravitated together, people such as Bill Stoneman, Don Whitehead, Jack Thompson, Clark Lee, Tex O'Reilly and myself.

We conjectured on when we would get the final call, conjectured on what assignments we would draw, for few of us knew what unit we would go with. And in more pensive moments we also conjectured on our chances of coming through alive.

We felt our chances were not very good. And we were not happy about it. Men like Don Whitehead and Clark Lee, who had been through the mill so long and so boldly, began to get nerves. And frankly I was the worst of the lot, and continued to be.

I began having terrible periods of depression and often would dream hideous dreams about it. All the time fear lay blackly deep upon our consciousness. It bore down on your heart like an all-consuming weight. People would talk to you and you wouldn't hear what they were saying.

The Army said they would try to give us 24 hours' notice of departure. Actually, the call came at 9 o'clock one morning and we were ordered to be at a certain place with full field kit at 10:30. We threw our stuff together. Some of us went away and left hotel rooms still running up bills. Many had dates that night but did not dare to phone and call them off.

As we arrived one by one at the appointed place, we looked both knowingly and sheepishly at each other. The Army continued to tell us that this was just another exercise, but we knew inside ourselves that this was it.

Bill Stoneman, who has been wounded once, never shows the slightest concern about these things. Whether he feels any concern or not I do not know. Bill has a humorous, sardonic manner. While we were waiting for the departure into the unknown, he took out a pencil and notebook as though starting to interview me.

'Tell me, Mr, Pyle, how does it feel to be an assault correspondent?'

Being a man of few words, I said, 'It feels awful.'

When everybody was ready, our luggage went into a truck and we went into jeeps. I can't tell you where we boarded the ship, of course, but I can say I personally rode two days in a jeep and made the last 30 miles on a 2 1/2-ton truck.

The first night we spent together at an assembly area, an Army tent camp. There, we drew our final battle kit - such things as clothing impregnated against gas attack, a shovel to dig foxholes, seasickness capsules, a carton of cigarets, a medical kit, rations and one funny little item which I can't mention but which was good for many purposes. We also drew three blankets just for the night, since our bedrolls had gone on ahead.

The weather was cold and three blankets were not enough. I hardly slept at all. When we awakened early the next morning,

Jack Thompson said, 'That's the coldest night I have ever spent.' Don Whitehead said, 'It's just as miserable as it always was.'

You see, we had all been living comfortably in hotels or apartments for the last few weeks. We had got a little soft, and here we were again starting back to the old horrible life we had known for so long - sleeping on the ground, only cold water, rations, foxholes, and dirt.

We were off to war again.

6/12/44
Normandy Beachhead[2]

Due to a last-minute alteration in the arrangements, I didn't arrive on the beachhead until the morning after D-day, after our first wave of assault troops had hit the shore.

By the time we got here, the beaches had been taken and the fighting had moved a couple of miles inland. All that remained on the beach was some sniping and artillery fire, and the occasional startling blast of a mine geysering brown sand into the air. That plus a gigantic and pitiful litter of wreckage along miles of shoreline.

Submerged tanks and overturned boats and burned trucks and shell-shattered jeeps and sad little personal belongings

---

2. In this long 'paper', Ernie Pyle describes the landings on Omaha Beach, even if the article was not named so. Why did he interrupt the story of his departure from England and his Channel crossing - one he had begun in his first article (and that he resumed in later ones)? Most likely because, after he had written and sent the first article, and was still aboard his ship, Ernie Pyle then landed in Normandy on 7th June. He afforded priority to current news, preferring to write his second article on the assault on 6th June, before returning to his story of the Channel crossing in following texts.

were strewn all over these bitter sands. That plus the bodies of soldiers lying in rows covered with blankets, the toes of their shoes sticking up in a line as though on drill. And other bodies, uncollected, still sprawling grotesquely in the sand or half hidden by the high grass beyond the beach.

That plus an intense, grim determination of work-weary men to get this chaotic beach organized and get all the vital supplies and the reinforcements moving more rapidly over it from the stacked-up ships standing in droves out to sea.

Now that it is over, it seems to me a pure miracle that we ever took the beach at all. For some of our units it was easy, but in this special sector where I am now, our troops faced such odds that our getting ashore was like my whipping Joe Louis[3] down to a pulp.

In this column, I want to tell you what the opening of the second front in this one sector entailed, so that you can know and appreciate and forever be humbly grateful to those both dead and alive who did it for you.

Ashore, facing us, were more enemy troops than we had in our assault waves. The advantages were all theirs, the disadvantages all ours. The Germans were dug into positions that they had been working on for months, although these were not yet all complete. A 100-foot bluff a couple of hundred yards back from the beach had great concrete gun emplacements built right into the hilltop. These opened to the sides instead of to the front, thus making it very hard for naval fire from the sea to reach them. They could shoot parallel with the beach and cover every foot of it for miles with artillery fire.

---

3. *Boxing world champion, heavyweight category, since 1937.*

Then they had hidden machine-gun nests on the forward slopes, with crossfire taking in every inch of the beach. These nests were connected by networks of trenches, so that the German gunners could move about without exposing themselves.

Throughout the length of the beach, running zigzag a couple of hundred yards back from the shoreline, was an immense V-shaped ditch 15 feet deep. Nothing could cross it, not even men on foot, until fills had been made. And in other places at the far end of the beach, where the ground is flatter, they had great concrete walls. These were blasted by our naval gunfire or by explosives set by hand after we got ashore.

Our only exits from the beach were several swales or valleys, each about 100 yards wide. The Germans made the most of these funnel-like traps, rowing them with buried mines. They contained, also, barbed-wire entanglements with mines attached, hidden ditches, and machine guns firing from the slopes.

This is what was on the shore. But our men had to go through a maze nearly as deadly as this before they even got ashore. Underwater obstacles were terrific. The Germans had whole fields of evil devices under the water to catch our boats. Even now, several days after the landing, we have cleared only channels through them and cannot yet approach the whole length of the beach with our ships. Even now, some ship or boat hits one of these mines every day and is knocked out of commission.

The Germans had masses of those great six-pronged spiders, made of railroad iron, and standing shoulder-high, just beneath the surface of the water for our landing craft to run into.

They also had huge logs buried in the sand, pointing upward and outward, their tops just below the water. Attached to these legs were mines.

In addition to these obstacles, they had floating mines offshore, land mines buried in the sand of the beach, and more mines in checkerboard rows in the tall grass beyond the sand. And the enemy had four men on shore for every three men we had approaching the shore.

And yet we got on.

Beach landings are planned to a schedule that is set far ahead of time. They all have to be timed, in order for everything to mesh and for the following waves of troops to be standing off the beach and ready to land at the right moment. As the landings are planned, some elements of the assault force are to break through quickly, push on inland, and attack the most obvious enemy strong points. It is usually the plan for units to be inland, attacking gun positions from behind, within a matter of minutes after the first men hit the beach.

I have always been amazed at the speed called for in these plans. You'll have schedules calling for engineers to land at H-hour plus two minutes, and service troops at H-hour plus 30 minutes, and even for press censors to land at H-hour plus 75 minutes. But in the attack on this special portion of the beach where I am - the worst we had, incidentally - the schedule didn't hold.

Our men simply could not get past the beach. They were pinned down right on the water's edge by an inhuman wall of fire from the bluff. Our first waves were on that beach for hours, instead of a few minutes before they could begin working inland.

You can still see the foxholes they dug at the very edge of the water, in the sand and the small, jumbled rocks that form parts of the beach.

Medical corpsmen attended the wounded as best they could. Men were killed as they stepped out of landing craft. An officer whom I knew got a bullet through the head just as the door of his landing craft was let down. Some men were drowned.

The first crack in the beach defenses was finally accomplished by terrific and wonderful naval gunfire, which knocked out the big emplacements, They tell epic stories of destroyers that ran right up into shallow water and had it out point-blank with the big guns in those concrete emplacements ashore.

When the heavy fire stopped, our men were organized by their officers and pushed on inland, circling machine-gun nests and taking them from the rear. As one officer said, the only way to take beach is to face it and keep going. It is costly at first, but it's the only way. If the men are pinned down on the beach, dug in and out of action, they might as well not be there at all. They hold up the waves behind them, and nothing is being gained.

Our men were pinned down for a while, but finally they stood up and went through and so we took that beach and accomplished our landing. We did it with every advantage on the enemy's side, and every disadvantage on ours. In the light of a couple of days of retrospection, we sit and talk and call it a miracle that our men ever got on at all or were able to stay on.

Before long it will be permitted to name the units that did it. Then you will know to whom this glory should go. They suffered casualties. And yet if you take the entire beachhead assault, including other units that had a much easier time, our total casualties in driving this wedge into the continent of Europe were remarkably low - only a fraction, in fact, of what our commanders had been prepared to accept.

And these units that were so battered and went through such hell are still, right at this moment pushing on inland without rest, their spirits high, their egotism in victory almost reaching the smart-alecky stage.

Their tails are up. 'We've done it again,' they say. They figure that the rest of the army isn't needed at all. Which proves that, while their judgment in this regard is bad, they certainly have the spirit that wins battles and eventually wars.

6/12/44
Normandy Beachhead

On our first morning after leaving London, the Army gave us assault correspondents a semifinal set of instructions and sent us off in jeeps in separate groups, each group to be divided up later until we were all separated.

We still weren't given any details of the coming invasion. We still didn't know where we were to go aboard ship, or what units we would be with.

As each batch left, the oldsters among us would shake hands. And because we weren't feeling very brilliant, almost our only words to each other were, 'Take it easy.'

The following morning, at another camp, I was called at 4 a.m. All around me officers were cussing and getting up. This was the headquarters of a certain outfit, and they were moving out in a motor convoy at dawn.

For months, these officers had been living a civilized existence, with good beds, good food, dress-up uniforms, polished desks and a normal social existence. But now, once again they were in battle clothes. They wore steel helmets and combat boots, and many carried packs on their backs.

They joked in the sleepy pre-dawn darkness. One said to another,

'What are you dressed up for, a masquerade?'

Everybody was overloaded with gear. One officer said, 'The Germans will have to come to us. We can never get to them with all this load.'

The most-repeated question, asked jokingly, was, 'Is your trip necessary?'

These men had spent months helping to plan this gigantic invasion. They were relieved to finish, the weary routine of paperwork at last, and glad to start putting their plans into action. If they had any personal concern about themselves, they didn't show it.

I rode with the convoy commander, who was an old friend. We were in an open jeep. It was just starting to get daylight when we pulled out. And just as we left it began raining - that dismal, cold, cruel rain that England is so capable of. It rained like that a year and a half ago when we left for Africa.

We drove all day. Motorcycles nursed each of our three sections along. We would halt every two hours for a stretch. At noon we opened K-rations. It was bitter cold.

Enlisted men had brought along a wire-haired terrier which belonged to one of the sergeants. We couldn't have an invasion without a few dogs along. At the rest halts, the terrier would get out in the fields to play and chase rocks with never any worry. It seemed wonderful to be a dog.

The English roads had been almost wholly cleared of normal traffic. British civil and army police were at every crossing. As we neared the embarkation point people along the roads stood at their doors and windows and smiled, 'bon voyage' to us. Happy children gave us the American o.k. sign - thumb and forefinger in a circle. One boy smilingly pointed a stick at us like a gun, and one of the soldiers pointed his rifle back and asked us with a grin,

'Shall I let him have it?'

One little girl, thinking the Lord knows what, made a nasty face at us.

Along toward evening we reached our ship. It was an LST[4], and it was already nearly loaded with trucks and armored cars and soldiers. Its ramp was down in the water, several yards from shore, and being an old campaigner I just waded aboard. But the officer behind me yelled up at the deck,

'Hey, tell the captain to move the ship up closer.'

So, they waited a few minutes, and the ramp was eased up onto dry ground, and our whole convoy walked aboard. Being an old campaigner, I was the only one in the crowd to get his feet wet.

We had hardly got aboard when the lines were cast off and we pulled out. That evening the colonel commanding the troops on our ship gave me the whole invasion plan in detail - the secret the whole world had waited years to hear, and once

---

4. *Landing Ship Tank.*

you have heard it, you become permanently a part of it. Now you were committed. It was too late to back out now, even if your heart failed you.

I asked a good many questions, and I realized my voice was shaking when I spoke but I couldn't help it. Yes, it would be tough, the colonel admitted. Our own part would be precarious. He hoped to go in with as few casualties as possible, but there would be casualties.

From a vague anticipatory dread, the invasion now turned into a horrible reality for me.

In a matter of hours, this holocaust of our own planning would swirl over us. No man could guarantee his own fate. It was almost too much for me. A feeling of utter desperation obsessed me throughout the night. It was nearly 4 a.m. before I got to sleep, and then it was a sleep harassed and torn by an awful knowledge.

6/14/44
Normandy Beachhead

On the way to the invasion, I rode an LST - the watery workhorse of this war. We carried armored reconnaissance troops.

We felt good about our position in the convoy, for we were about a third of the way back in the column. That meant we had ships on all sides of us and we wouldn't be on the outside in case of attack.

Our convoy was made up entirely of LST's. Each of us towed a big steel pontoon section, there to be used as barges and docks in the shallow waters along the beach. And behind each pontoon we also towed a smaller pontoon with two huge outboard motors on it - a thing called a 'rhino'[5].

Several ships broke cables and lost their pontoons during the journey. Special Coast Guard tugs were assigned to pick them up. We lost our own rhino on the last night out, and I don't know whether it was picked up or not.

We were told that, if the ship sank, our chances of being picked up would be slight. The water was so cold we would lose consciousness in 15 minutes and die within four hours.

So, we all conjectured about the possibility of clambering out onto the trailing pontoon if the ship went down. That brought up the question whether the pontoon would be cut loose if the ship sank or be dragged under the water by its huge steel table.

To show how rumors get around, one soldier said he had learned that the ship had a sailor standing aft with an ax, for the sole purpose of hacking the cable in two if the ship were torpedoed. Later, I asked the captain and he said there wasn't any such man at all.

Funny little things happen in a convoy. The steering gear on one ship broke in mid-afternoon and the ship came slowly careening around like a skidding automobile until it was crosswise of the convoy and the ships behind had to veer around it.

You see, we were lined up in straight columns, extending as far ahead and behind as we could see. On both sides of us ran

---

5. As indicated by Ernie Pyle, the Rhino Ferries were motorised barges that were used to unload the LSTs anchored off the Landing Beaches. Once loaded, the Rhino Ferries transported their cargo to dry land.

destroyers and corvettes for escort but, as I've said before, it never seems to the participants in a convoy that the escort is adequate.

Our only scare came late in the night before we hit the invasion area. I was in my bunk, and the colonel with whom I was rooming came down from the bridge.

'How are things going?' I asked.

'Terrible,' he said. 'Another convoy came along and pushed us out of the swept channel. One engine has broken clear down and the other can only run at third speed. The wind and tide are drifting us toward the Belgian coast. We're steering straight west but barely holding our direction.'

I thought how ironic it would be to wind up this war by drifting alone onto a hostile beach and spending the rest of the war in a prison camp - if we didn't hit a mine first. But fortunately, I was too sleepy to worry about it. When I awakened at dawn, we had both engines going and were back in line again in the swept channel. Moral: always be too sleepy to give a damn.

My own devastating sense of fear and depression, of which I have spoken before, disappeared the moment we were underway. As I write this, the old familiar crack and roar of big guns is all around us, and the beach is a great brown haze of smoke and dust, and we know that bombers will be over us tonight. Yet all that haunting premonition, that soul-consuming dread, is gone and the war is prosaic to me again. And I believe that is true of everyone aboard, even those who have never been in combat before.

The night before sailing we were instructed to take two anti-seasickness capsules before breakfast the next day and follow them up with one every four hours throughout the voyage. The capsules had been issued to us with our battle kits.

Well, we took the first two and they almost killed us. The capsules have a strong sleeping powder in them, and by noon all the Army personnel aboard were in a drugged stupor. Fortunately, the Navy, being proud, didn't take any, so somebody was left to run the ship.

The capsules not only put us to sleep but they constricted our throats, made our mouths bone-dry and dilated the pupils of our eyes until we could hardly see.

When we recovered from this insidious jag, along toward evening, we all threw our seasickness medicine away, and after that we felt fine. Although the Channel crossing was rough, I didn't hear of a single man aboard our ship who got sick.

6/15/44
Normandy Beachhead

The ship on which I rode to the invasion of the Continent brought certain components of the second wave of assault troops. We arrived in the congested waters of the beachhead shortly after dawn on D-One Day.

We aboard this ship had secretly dreaded the trip, for we had expected attacks from U-boats, E-boats and, at nighttime, from aircraft. Yet nothing whatever happened.

We were at sea for a much longer time than it would ordinarily take to make a bee-line journey from England to France. The convoy we sailed in was one of several which comprised what is known as a 'force.' As we came down, the English Channel was crammed with forces going both ways and, as I write, it still is. Minesweepers had swept wide channels for us, all the way from England to France. These were marked with buoys. Each channel was miles wide.

We surely saw, there before us, more ships than any human had ever seen before at one glance. And going north were other vast convoys, some composed of fast liners speeding back to England for new loads of troops and equipment.

As far as you could see in every direction, the ocean was infested with ships. There must have been every type of ocean-going vessel in the world. I even thought I saw a paddlewheel steamer in the distance, but that was probably an illusion.

There were battleships and all other kinds of warships clear down to patrol boats. There were great fleets of Liberty Ships. There were fleets of luxury liners turned into troop transports, and fleets of big landing craft and tank carriers and tankers. And in and out through it all were nondescript ships - converted yachts, river boats, tugs, and barges.

The best way I can describe this vast armada and the frantic urgency of the traffic is to suggest that you visualize New York Harbor on its busiest day of the year and then just enlarge that scene until it takes in all the ocean the human eye can reach, clear around the horizon. And over the horizon there are dozens of times that many.

We were not able to go ashore immediately after arriving off the invasion coast amidst the great pool of ships in what was known as the 'transport area.'

Everything is highly organized in an invasion and every ship, even the tiniest one, is always under exact orders timed to the minute. But, at one time, our convoy was so pushed along by the wind and the currents that we were five hours ahead of schedule, despite the fact that our engines had been stopped half the time. We lost this by circling.

Although we arrived just on time, they weren't ready for us on the beaches and we spent several hours weaving in and out among the multitude of ships just off the beachhead, and finally just settled down to await our turn.

That was when the most incongruous - to us - part of the invasion came. Here we were in a front-row seat at a great military epic. Shells from battleships were whamming over our heads, and occasionally a dead man floated face downward past us. Hundreds and hundreds of ships laden with death milled around us. We could stand at the rail and see both our shells and German shells exploding on the beaches, where struggling men were leaping ashore, desperately hauling guns and equipment in through the water.

We were in the very vortex of the war - and yet, as we sat there waiting, Lieut. Chuck Conick and I played gin rummy in the wardroom and Bing Crosby sang, 'Sweet Leilani' over the ship's phonograph.

Angry shells hitting near us would make heavy thuds as the concussion carried through the water and struck the hull of our ship. But in our wardroom men in gas-impregnated uniforms and wearing lifebelts sat reading *Life* and listening to the BBC telling us how the war before our eyes was going.

But it isn't like that ashore. No, it isn't like that ashore.

The terrible waste of war

6/16/44
Normandy Beachhead

D-Day Plus two. I took a walk along the historic coast of Normandy in the country of France. It was a lovely day for strolling along the seashore. Men were sleeping on the sand, some of them sleeping forever. Men were floating in the water, but they didn't know they were in the water for they were dead.

The water was full of squishy little jellyfish about the size of your hand. Millions of them. In the center, each of them had a green design exactly like a four-leaf clover. The good luck emblem.

Sure. Hell yes.

I walked for a mile and a half along the water's edge of our many-miled invasion beach. You wanted to walk slowly, for the detail on that beach was infinite.

The wreckage was vast and startling. The awful waste and destruction of war, even aside from the loss of human life, has always been one of its outstanding features to those who are in it. Anything and everything is expendable. And we did expend on our beachhead in Normandy during those first few hours.

For a mile out from the beach, there were scores of tanks and trucks and boats that you could no longer see, for they were at the bottom of the water - swamped by overloading, or hit by shells, or sunk by mines. Most of their crews were lost.

You could see trucks tipped half over and swamped. You could see partly sunken barges, and the angled-up corners of jeeps, and small landing craft half submerged. And at low tide you could still see those vicious six pronged-iron snares that helped snag and wreck them.

On the beach itself, high and dry, were all kinds of wrecked vehicles. There were tanks that had only just made the beach before being knocked out. There were jeeps that had burned to a dull gray. There were big derricks on caterpillar treads that didn't quite make it. There were half-tracks carrying office equipment that had been made into a shambles by a single shell hit, their interiors still holding their useless equipage of smashed typewriters, telephones, office files.

There were LCT's turned completely upside down and lying on their backs, and how they got that way I don't know. There were boats stacked on top of each other their sides caved in, their suspension doors knocked off.

In this shoreline museum of carnage, there were abandoned rolls of barbed wire and smashed bulldozers and big stacks of thrown away lifebelts and piles of shells still waiting to be moved.

In the water floated empty life rafts and soldiers' packs and ration boxes, and mysterious oranges.

On the beach lay snarled rolls of telephone wire and big rolls of steel matting and stacks of broken, rusting rifles.

On the beach lay, expended, sufficient men and mechanism for a small war. They were gone forever now. And yet we could afford it.

We could afford it because we were on, we had our toehold, and behind us there were such enormous replacements for this wreckage on the beach that you could hardly conceive of their sum total. Men and equipment were flowing from England in such a gigantic stream that it made the waste on the beachhead seem like nothing at all, really nothing at all.

A few hundred yards back on the beach is a high bluff. Up there we had a tent hospital, and a barbed-wire enclosure for prisoners of war. From up there you could see far up and down the beach, in a spectacular crow's nest view, and far out to sea.

And standing out there on the water beyond all this wreckage was the greatest armada man has ever seen. You simply could not believe the gigantic collection of ships that lay out there waiting to unload.

Looking from the bluff, it lay thick and clear to the far horizon of the sea and on beyond, and it spread out to the sides and was miles wide. Its utter enormity would move the hardest man.

As I stood up there, I noticed a group of freshly taken German prisoners standing nearby. They had not yet been put in the prison cage. They were just standing there, a couple of doughboys leisurely guarding them with Tommy guns.

The prisoners too were looking out to sea - the same bit of sea that for months and years had been so safely empty before their gaze. Now they stood staring almost as if in a trance.

They didn't say a word to each other. They didn't need to. The expression on their faces was something forever unforgettable. In it was the final horrified acceptance of their doom.

If only all Germany could have had the rich experience of standing on the bluff and looking out across the water and seeing what their compatriots saw.

A great and narrow fringe of sadness

6/17/44
Normandy Beachhead

In the preceding column, we told about the D-Day wreckage among our machines of war that were expended in taking one of the Normandy beaches.

But there is another and more human litter. It extends in a thin little line, just like a high-water mark, for miles along the beach. This is the strewn personal gear, gear that will never be needed again, of those who fought and died to give us our entrance into Europe.

Here in a jumbled row for mile on mile are soldiers' packs. Here are socks and shoe polish, sewing kits, diaries, Bibles and hand grenades. Here are the latest letters from home, with the address on each one neatly razored out - one of the security precautions enforced before the boys embarked.

Here are toothbrushes and razors, and snapshots of families back home staring up at you from the sand. Here are pocketbooks, metal mirrors, extra trousers, and bloody, abandoned shoes. Here are broken-handled shovels, and portable radios smashed almost beyond recognition, and mine detectors twisted and ruined.

Here are torn pistol belts and canvas water buckets, first aid kits and jumbled heaps of lifebelts. I picked up a pocket Bible with a soldier's name in it and put in in my jacket. I carried it half a mile or so and then put it back down on the beach. I don't know why I picked it up, or why I put it back down.

Soldiers carry strange things ashore with them. In every invasion, you'll find at least one soldier hitting the beach at H-Hour with a banjo slung over his shoulder. The most ironic piece of equipment marking our beach - this beach of first despair, then victory - is a tennis racket that some soldier had brought along. It lies lonesomely on the sand, clamped in its rack, not a string broken.

Two of the most dominant items in the beach refuse are cigarets and writing paper. Each soldier was issued a carton of cigarets just before he started. Today, these cartons by the thousand, watersoaked and spilled out, mark the line of our first savage blow.

Writing paper and airmail envelopes come second. The boys had intended to do a lot of writing in France. Letters that would have filled those blank, abandoned pages.

Always there are dogs in every invasion. There is a dog still on the beach today pitifully looking for his masters.

He stays at the water's edge, near a boat that lies twisted and half sunk at the waterline. He barks appealingly to every soldier who approaches, trots eagerly along with him for a few feet, and then, sensing himself unwanted in all this haste, runs back to wait in vain for his own people at his own empty boat.

Over and around this long thin line of personal anguish, fresh men today are rushing vast supplies to keep our armies pushing on into France. Other squads of men pick amidst the wreckage to salvage ammunition and equipment that are still usable.

Men worked and slept on the beach for days before the last D-Day victim was taken away for burial.

I stepped over the form of one youngster whom I thought dead. But when I looked down, I saw he was only sleeping. He was very young, and very tired. He lay on one elbow, his hand suspended in the air about six inches from the ground. And in the palm of hand, he held a large, smooth rock.

I stood and looked at him a long time. He seemed in his sleep to hold that rock lovingly, as though it were his last link with a vanishing world. I have no idea at all why he went to sleep with the

rock in his hand, or what kept him from dropping it once he was asleep. It was just one of those little things without explanation that a person remembers for a long time.

The strong, swirling tides of the Normandy coastline shift the contours of the sandy beach as they move in and out. They carry soldiers' bodies out to sea, and later they return them. They cover the corpses of heroes with sand, and then in their whims they uncover them. As I plowed out over the wet sand of the beach on that first day ashore, I walked around what seemed to be a couple of pieces of driftwood sticking out of the sand. But they weren't driftwood.

They were a soldier's two feet. He was completely covered by the shifting sands except for his feet. The toes of his G.I. shoes pointed toward the land he had come so far to see, and which he saw so briefly.

06/19/44
Normandy Beachhead

When I went ashore on the soil of France, the first thing I wanted to do was hunt up the other correspondents. I had said goodbye to a few days previously in England, and see how they had fared. Before the day of invasion, we had accepted it as a fact that not everybody would come through alive.

We have little information on this picture where we can see Ernie Pyle (2nd from the left) using a spade to dig out a foxhole. All we know is that it was taken in Vouilly, in Calvados. From 10 June to 10 August 1944, the Château de Vouilly served as the American press camp and reunited all the journalists following the GIs in Normandy. It was in Vouilly that the daily press conferences organised by the American military staff were held. © *Photo Indiana State Museum*

Correspondents sort of gang together. They know the ins and in outs of war, and they all work at it in much the same manner. So, I knew about where to look, and I didn't have much trouble finding them.

It was early in the morning, before the boys had started out on their day's round of covering war. I found them in foxholes dug into the rear slope of a grassy hill about a half-mile from the beach. I picked them out from a distance, because I could spot Jack Thompson's beard. He was sitting on the edge of a foxhole lacing his paratrooper boots. About a dozen correspondents were there, among them three especially good friends of mine – Thompson, Don Whitehead and Tex O'Reilly.

First of all, we checked with each other on what we had heard about other correspondents. Most of them were OK One had been killed, and one was supposed to have been lost on a sunken ship, but we didn't know who. One or two had been wounded. Three of our best friends had not been heard from at all, and it looked bad, but they have since turned up safe.

The boys were unshaven, and their eyes were red. Their muscles were stiff and their bodies ached. They had carried ashore only their typewriters and some K-rations. They had gone two days without sleep, and then had slept on the ground without blankets, in wet clothes.

But none of that mattered too much after what they had been through. They were in a sort of daze from the exhaustion and mental turmoil of battle. When you asked a question, it would take them a few seconds to focus their thoughts and give you an answer.

Two of them in particular had been through all the frightful nightmare that the assault troops had experienced - because they had come ashore with them.

Don Whitehead hit the beach with one regiment just an hour after H-Hour, Thompson at the same time with another regiment. They were on the beaches for more than four hours under that hideous burst of sheds and bullets.

Jack Thompson said, 'You've never seen a beach like it before. Dead and wounded men were lying so thick you could hardly take a step. One officer was killed only two feet away from me.'

Whitehead was still asleep when I went to his foxhole. I said, 'Get up, you lazy so-and-so.' He started grinning without even opening his eyes, for he knew who it was.

It was hard for him to wake up. He had been unable to sleep, from sheer exhaustion, and had taken a sleeping tablet.

Don had managed to steal one blanket on the beach and had that wrapped around him. He had taken off his shoes for the first time in two days. His feet were so sore from walking in wet shoes and socks that he had to give them some air.

Finally, he began to get himself up. 'I don't know why I'm alive at all,' he said. 'It was really awful. For hours, there on the beach, the shells were so close that they were throwing mud and rocks all over you. It was so bad that after a while you didn't care whether you got hit or not.'

Don fished in a cardboard ration box for some cigarets. He pulled out an envelope and threw it into the bushes. 'They ain't worth a damn,' he said. The envelope contained his anti-seasickness tablets.

'I was sicker than hell while we were circling around in our landing craft waiting to come ashore,' he said. 'Everybody was sick. Soldiers were lying on the floor of the LCVP sick as dogs.'

Tex O'Reilly rode around in a boat for six hours waiting to get ashore. Everybody was wet and cold and seasick and scared. War is so romantic - if you're far away from it.

Whitehead has probably been in more amphibious landings than any other correspondent over here. I know of six he has made, four of them murderously tough. And he said,

'I think I have gone on one too many of these things. Not because of what might happen to me personally, but I have lost my perspective. It's like dreaming the same nightmare over and over again, and when you try to write you feel that you have written it all before. You can't think of any new or different words to say it with.' I know only too well what he means.

It is an ironic thing about correspondents who go in on the first few days of an invasion story. They are the only correspondents capable of telling the full and intimate drama and horror of the thing. And yet they are the ones who can't get their copy out to the world.

By the time they do get it out, events have swirled on and the world doesn't care anymore.

There that morning in their foxholes on the slope of the hill, those correspondents were mainly worried about the communications situation. Forty-eight hours after H-hour, correspondents who had landed with the first wave felt sure that none of their copy had ever reached America. And even I, a day behind them, feel no assurance that these feeble essays of mine will ever see the light of day. But in philosophical moments I can think of greater catastrophes than that.

06/20/44
Somewhere in France

Would you be interested in hearing how we spent our first night in France? Well, even if you wouldn't...

Just after supper, we got an order to unload our vehicles from the LST. One of those big self-propelled bargelike things, made of steel pontoons bolted together, came up in front of our ship and the vehicles were driven off onto it.

These barges are called rhinos. They move very slowly and it took us an hour to get to shore. Then the beachmaster signaled us not to land, for the tide wasn't right. So, we had to loaf around out there on the water for another hour.

They were blowing up mines on the beach, and some of our big naval guns were still thundering away at the Germans. The evening was cloudy and miserable, and it began to rain as we waited. We were all cold.

At last the beachmaster let us in. The barge grounded about fifty yards from shore, and runways were let down.

Every one of our vehicles had been waterproofed, so that the engines wouldn't drown out while going through the surf.

I came ashore in a jeep with Pvt. William Bates Wescott, of (4040 W. Boulevard) Culver City, Cal. Wescott is a good-looking, intelligent man of 26 who used to be a salesman for the Edgemar Farms Dairy at Venice, Cal. He is at war for the first time, and all this shooting and stuff are completely new to him, but he is going all right.

Wescott's wife works in downtown Los Angeles, and just in case you want to take her some flowers for being the wife of such a nice guy, she's the girl who makes Pullman reservations for the Southern Pacific Railroad at Sixth and Main.

Wescott and I were the first ones off the barge. I had waterproofed my typewriter by taping it up in a gas cape. But the water came only to the floor of the jeep. We didn't even get our feet wet, but the waves did slosh in and get the seats of our pants wet.

It was several miles to our bivouac area. On the way we passed many bodies lying alongside the road, both German and American but mostly German. Some of the French people along the road smiled and waved, while others kept their heads down and wouldn't look up.

It was dark when we got to our bivouac, a grape and apple orchard on a hillside. We pulled in and parked under a tree. First, we posted sentries, and then Wescott dug into his big ration box in the jeep and got out some grapefruit juice, crackers and sardines.

While we were eating, the first German planes of the night came over. One dropped its bombs not awfully far away - enough to give us our first touch of nerves. There were antiaircraft guns all around and they made an awful racket. The night began to take on an ominous and spooky aspect. We felt lonely. There were still snipers around, and shell holes everywhere, and we could hear machine guns in the distance.

It was midnight by the time we had finished eating and got a camouflage net over the jeep in preparation for the first light next morning. We decided to get what sleep we could. We didn't have our bedrolls yet, but we did have two blankets apiece. We just lay down on the ground.

Another jeep had pulled under the tree with us. Altogether our little group sleeping on the ground consisted of two colonels, three enlisted men and myself. We slept in all our clothes.

German planes kept coming over one by one. Our guns kept up their booming and crackling all night long, in fits and jerks.

After an hour or so, one of our colonels said we'd better move our blankets so our heads would be under the jeeps, because pieces of flak were falling all over the orchard.

He said the flak wouldn't kill you unless it hit you in the head. I said I guessed it would if it hit you in the stomach. He said it wouldn't. I still think it would.

Anyhow, I moved my head under and left my stomach out in the open. My head was right behind the front wheel under the fender. It was a good place, but the headroom was so scant that every time I would turn over, I would get a mouthful of mud from the tender.

Then we got cold. Our two blankets might as well have been handkerchiefs, for all the warmth there was in them. We lit cigarets and smoked under our blankets. We couldn't sleep much anyhow, for the noise of the guns.

Sometimes planes would come in low, and we would lie there scrunched up in that knotty tenseness you get when waiting to be hit.

Finally, daylight came. At dawn our planes always come over and the Germans leave, so the days are safe and secure as far as the air is concerned.

We all got up at dawn, welcoming a chance to move around and get warm. Private Wescott opened some K-rations and we ate a scanty breakfast off the hood of the jeep. Then a colonel made a reconnaissance tour. When he came back, he said that our little orchard, which looked so rural and pretty in the dawn, was full of dead Germans, killed the day before. We would have to help bury them pretty soon. That was our first night in France.

The lighter side of things

6/21/44
Somewhere in France

The war is constantly producing funny things as well as tragic things, so I might as well tell you some of our lighter incidents.

For example, the first night we spent in France one of the colonels who slept with us under an apple tree was an Army observer from Washington. Usually, we don't care for observers from Washington, but this colonel was a very nice guy and a good field soldier too, and everybody liked him.

While we were eating our K-rations next morning, he said he had slept fine for the first hour, before we had moved in under our jeep for protection from the flak. He said that before we moved, he had found a nice little mound of earth to put his head on for a pillow.

He said that all his life he had had to have a pillow of some kind. After moving under the jeep, he couldn't find anything to put his head on.

With that he walked over a few feet to show us the nice mound of earth. When he looked down, he started laughing. His excellent pillow of the night before had turned out in the light of day to be a pile of horse manure.

***

Another story concerns a masterful piece of wartime understatement by one of our truck drivers, Pvt. Carl Vonhorn, of RFD No. 2, Cooperstown, N.Y. He had pulled into an apple orchard adjoining ours the night before, parked his truck in the darkness, spread his blankets on the ground in front of the truck, and gone to sleep.

When he woke up at daylight, Vonhorn looked about him sleepily. And there on the ground right beside him, within arm's reach, was a dead German soldier. And when he looked on the other side, there, equally close, were two potato-mashers (hand grenades). Private Vonhorn got up very quickly.

Later he was telling his officers about his startling experience, and he ended his description with this philosophical remark, 'It was very distasteful.'

Everybody thought that was so funny it spread around the camp like fire, and now the phrase, 'It's very distasteful,' has become practically a by-word.

***

After breakfast that first morning, we had to round up about 50 dead Germans and Americans in the series of orchards where we were camping and carry them to a central spot in a pasture and bury them.

I helped carry one corpse across a couple of fields. I did it partly because the group needed an extra man, and partly because I was forcing myself to get used to it, for you can't hide from death when you're in a war.

This German was just a kid, surely not over 15. His face had already turned black, but you could sense his youth through the death-distorted features.

The boys spread a blanket on the ground beside him. Then we lifted him over onto it. One soldier and I each took hold of a foot, and two others took his arms. One of the two soldiers in front was hesitant about touching the corpse. Whereupon the other soldier said to him,

'Go on, take hold of him, dammit. You might as well get used to it now, for you'll be carrying plenty of dead ones from now on. Hell, you may even be carrying me one of these days.'

So, we carried him across two fields, each of us holding a corner of the blanket. Our burden got pretty heavy, and we rested a couple of times. The boys made wisecracks along the way to cover up their distaste for the job.

When we got to the field, we weren't sure just where the lieutenant wanted the cemetery started. So, we put our man down on the ground and went back for instructions. And as we walked away, the funny guy of the group turned and shook a finger at the dead German and said,

'Now don't you run away while we're gone.'

***

The Germans leave snipers behind when they retreat, so all American bivouac areas are heavily guarded by sentries at night. And the sentries really mean business.

The other night, a pretty important general whom I know was working late, as all our staff officers do these days. About midnight, he left his tent to go to another general's tent and talk something over.

He had gone only about 20 feet when a sentry challenged him. And just at that moment the general, groping around in the dark, fell headlong into a deep slit trench. It was funny, even to the general, but there was nothing humorous about it to the sentry. He suspected monkey business. He rushed up to the trench, pointed his gun at the general, and in a tone that was a mixture of terror and intent to kill he yelled, 'Git out of there and git recognized, you!'

The European Campaign explained

6/22/44
Somewhere in France

Folks newly arrived from America say that you people at home are grave and eager about this, our greatest operation of the war so far.

But they say also that you are giving the landings themselves an importance out of proportion to what must follow before the war can end. They say you feel that now that we are on the soil of France, we will just sweep rapidly ahead and the Germans will soon crumble.

It is natural for you to feel that, and nobody is blaming you. But I thought maybe in this column I could help your understanding of things if we sort of charted this European campaign. This is no attempt to predict, it is just an effort to clarify.

On the German side in Western Europe, we face an opponent who has been building his defenses and his forces for four years. A great army of men was here waiting for us, well prepared and well equipped.

On the English side of the Channel, we and the British spent more than two years building up to equality in men and arms with this opponent. Finally, we reached that equality, and I am sure considerably, more than equality.

Then - on June 6 - came the invasion we had waited for so long. 'The big show has begun. So, let's divide the remainder of this campaign into phases.'

Phase No. 1 was the highly vital task of getting ashore at all. That phase could not last long. We either had to break a hole in the beach defenses and have our men flowing through that hole within a few hours, or the jig was up. Phase No. 1 came out all in our favor.

We planned Phase No. 2 so that we could throw in our first follow-up waves without casualties or delay. That also was a phase we didn't dare to dilly-dally about. The beaches were fairly clear of shellfire within two days.

Phase No. 3 is what we are in right now. And that is to build a wall of troops around the outer rim of our beachhead that will hold off any German counter-attacks.

The whole split-second question of the first few days was whether we could get troops and supplies through our little needle's eye of a beachhead faster than the Germans could bring theirs from all over Europe.

As this is written no important counter-attack has developed. The Germans are having plenty of trouble moving their stuff up, because of our savage air activity. Every day that passes adds to our forces and gives us greater security.

If we can hold that outer line against all attack for a short while yet, then we will have won Phase No. 3. And right now, it certainly seems that we are winning it.

Phases 1, 2 and 3 were all preliminary ones. It took three of them merely to get us a place in Europe from which to begin. The three of them merely give us the corner lot on which we are going to build our house.

Phase No. 4 is the house-building phase. This is the phase you folks at home have been working so hard to make possible.

In England and America, we've got the men and machines and supplies and munitions to overbalance the great stockpile Germany has built up in Western Europe. But we've got to get it over here into France before we go on.

You may have imagined that we would hit the beach and go right on, advancing 30 miles a day, till we reached the German border. We could no more do that than a baby, after taking its first step, could run a hundred-yard dash. You have to wait until your strength is built up before you can run.

That is Phase No. 4. It will go on for some time yet. Don't be impatient. The wall in front of us will hold while we gradually pile this beachhead to the saturation point with extra men, guns, trucks, food, ammunition, gasoline, telephone wire, repair shops, hospitals, airfields, and thousands of other items - pack it until we have more than the Germans have, and with lots of reserves in addition.

Then and not until then will Phase No. 5 start. Phase No. 5 is the real war, big-scale war. How long we will have to wait between now and the beginning of Phase No. 5, I don't know. But my guess is that it will take months rather than weeks.

Naturally, there will be fighting during that time, The Germans will try to crush us back onto the beaches. We at the same time try to extend our holdings enough to protect our accumulating men and supplies.

But Phase No. 5 will be the final one. How long it will last, I also don't know - and in that ignorance I have a great deal of company. I doubt if anyone in the world knows. All we do know is that things look good and that it will definitely end in our favor.

So don't be impatient if we seem to go slowly for a while. You can't lay the foundation of a house in the forenoon and move into the house that evening. We are just now laying the foundation of our house of war in Europe. It will take a while to build the walls and get the roof on. And then...

A tour of the peninsula

6/23/44
On the Cherbourg Peninsula

The day after troops of our Ninth division pushed through and cut off this peninsula[6] I went touring in a jeep over the country they had just taken.

This Norman country is truly lovely in many places. Here in the western part of the peninsula the ground becomes hilly and rolling. Everything is a vivid green, there are trees everywhere, and the view across the fields from a rise looks exactly like the rich, gentle land of eastern Pennsylvania. It is too wonderfully beautiful to be the scene of war, and yet so were parts of Tunisia and Sicily and Italy. Some day, I would like to cover a war in a country that is as ugly as war itself.

Our ride was a sort of spooky one. The American troops had started north and were driving on Cherbourg. This was possible because the Germans in that section were thoroughly disorganized, and by now capable of nothing more than trying to escape.

There was no traffic whatever on the roads. You could drive for miles without seeing a soul. We had been told that the country was still full of snipers, and we knew there were batches of Germans in the woods waiting to surrender. And yet we saw nothing. The beautiful, tree-bordered lanes were empty. Cattle grazed contentedly in the fields. It was as though life had

---

6. *The Cotentin peninsula was cut by the American troups level with Barneville on 18 June 1944.*

taken a holiday and death was in hiding. It gave you the willies.

Finally, we came to a stone schoolhouse which was being used as a prisoner-of-war collection point, so we stopped for a look. Here groups of prisoners were constantly being brought in. And here individual American soldiers who had been cut off behind the lines for days came wearily to rest for a while in the courtyard before going on back to hunt up their outfits.

Most of the prisoners coming in at the time were from a captured German hospital. German doctors had set up shop in a shed adjoining the school and were treating their prisoners, who had slight wounds. At the moment I walked up, one soldier had his pants down and a doctor was probing for a fragment in his hip.

Two or three of the German officers spoke some English. They were in a very good humor. One of them, a doctor, said to me, 'I've been in the army four years, and today is the best day I have spent in the army.'

In this courtyard, I ran onto two boys who had just walked back after losing their jeep and being surrounded for hours that morning by Germans.

They were Pfc. Arthur MacDonald, of Portsmouth, N.H., and Pvt. T.C. McFarland, of Southern Pines, N.C. They were forward observers for the Ninth Division's artillery.

They had bunked down the night before in a pasture. When they woke up, they could hear voices all around, and they weren't American voices. They peeked out and saw a German at a latrine not 30 feet away.

So, they started crawling. They crawled for hours. Finally, they got out of the danger zone, and they started walking. They met a French farmer along the road and took him in tow.

'We sure captured that Frenchman,' they said. 'He was so scared he could hardly talk. We used high-school French and a dictionary and finally got it through his head that all we wanted was something to eat. So, he took us to his house. He fried eggs and pork and made coffee for us.

'Our morale sure was low this morning but that Frenchman we captured fixed it up.'

The boys pulled out a couple of snapshots of the Frenchman, and they were so grateful that I imagine they will carry those pictures the rest of their lives.

At this time the French in that vicinity had been 'liberated' less than 12 hours, and they could hardly encompass it in their minds. They were relieved, but they hardly knew what to do.

As we left the prison enclosure and got into our jeep, we noticed four or five French country people - young farmers in their 20s, I would take them to be - leaning against a nearby house.

As we sat in the jeep getting our gear adjusted, one of the farmers walked toward us, rather hesitantly and timidly. But finally, he came up and smilingly handed me a rose.

I couldn't go around carrying a rose in my hand all afternoon, so I threw it away around the next bend. But little things like that do sort of make you feel good about the human race.

When the Evangile of good-willed men thundered through the skies

6/24/44
Barneville, Normandy

From this picturesque little town, you can look down upon the western sea. In the center of Barneville is a sloping, paved court, a sort of public square except that it is rectangular instead of square.

At one end of the square, an Army truck was parked. Scattered around the square were half a dozen American soldiers standing in doorways with their rifles at the ready. There are a few French people on the streets.

We went to the far end of the square where three local French policemen were standing in front of the mayor's office. They couldn't speak any English, but they said there was one woman in town who did, and a little boy was sent running for her. Gradually, a crowd of eager and curious people crushed in upon us, until there must have been 200 of them, from babies to old women.

Finally, the woman arrived - a little dark woman with graying hair, and spectacles, and a big smile. Her English was quite good, and we asked her if there were any Germans in the town. She turned and asked the policemen.

Instantly everybody in the crowd started talking at once. The sound was like that of a machine that increases in speed until its noise drowns out all else.

Finally, the policemen had to shush the crowd so the woman could answer us. She said there were Germans all around, in the woods, but none whatever left in the town. Just then a German stuck his head out of a nearby second-story window. Somebody saw him, and an American soldier was dispatched to get him.

Barneville is a fortunate place, because not a shell was fired into it by either side, The lieutenant with us told the woman we were glad nobody had been hurt. When she translated this for the crowd, there was much nodding in approval of our good wishes.

We must have stood and talked for an hour and a half. It was a kind of holiday for the local people. They were relieved but still not quite sure the Germans wouldn't be back. They were still under a restraint that wouldn't let them open up riotously. But you could sense from little things that they were glad to have us,

A little French shopkeeper came along with a spool of red, white and blue ribbon from his store. He cut off pieces about six inches long for all hands, both American and French. In a few minutes, everybody was going around with a French tri-color in his buttonhole.

Then a ruddy-faced man of middle age, who looked like a gentleman farmer drove up in one of those one-horse, high-wheeled work carts that the French use.

He had a German prisoner in uniform standing behind him, and another one, who was sick, lying on a stretcher. The farmer had captured these guys himself, and he looked so pleased with himself that I expected him to take a bow at any moment.

French people kept coming up and asking us for instructions. A man who looked as if he might be the town banker asked what he was supposed to do with prisoners.

We told him to bring them to the truck and asked how many he had. To our astonishment he said he had 70 in the woods a couple of miles away, 120 in a nearby town, and 40 in another town. As far as I could figure it out, he had captured them all himself.

Another worried-looking Frenchman came up. He was a doctor. He said he had 26 badly wounded Germans down at the railroad station and desperately needed medical supplies. He wanted chloroform and sulfa drugs. We told him we would have some sent.

One character in the crowd looked as if he belonged in a novel of Bohemian life on the left bank in Paris. He couldn't possibly have been anything but a poet. He wore loose, floppy clothes that made him look like a woman. His glasses were thick, and hair about a foot long curled around his ears. I wish you could have seen the expressions of our tough, dirty soldiers when they looked at him.

When we finally started away from the crowd, a little old fellow in faded blue overalls ran up and asked us, in sign language, to come to his cafe for a drink. Since we didn't dare violate the spirit of hands-across-the-sea that was then wafting about the town, we had to sacrifice ourselves and accept.

So, we sat on wooden benches at a long bare table while the little Frenchman puttered and sputtered around. He let two policemen and his own family in, and then took the handle out of the front door so nobody else could get in.

The Germans had drunk up all his stock except for some wine and some eau de vie. In case you don't know, eau de vie is a savage liquid made by boiling barbed wire, soapsuds, watch springs and old tent pegs together. The better brands have a touch of nitroglycerine for flavor.

So, the little Frenchman filled our tiny glasses. We raised them, touched glasses all around, and vived la France all over the place, and good-will-towards-men rang out through the air and tears ran down our cheeks.

In this case, however, the tears were largely induced by our violent efforts to refrain from clutching at our throats and crying out in anguish. This good-will business is a tough life, and I think every American who connects with a glass of eau de vie should get a Purple Heart[7].

---

7. *The Purple Heart is a military decoration awarded to American soldiers killed or wounded in combat.*

Hedgerow warfare

6/26/44
Somewhere in France

Sniping, as far as I know, is recognized as a legitimate means of warfare. And yet there is something sneaking about it that outrages the American sense of fairness.

I had never sensed this before we landed in France and began pushing the Germans back. We have had snipers before - in Bizerte[8] and Cassino[9] and lots of other places. But always on a small scale.

Here in Normandy the Germans have gone in for sniping in a wholesale manner. There are snipers everywhere. There are snipers in trees, in buildings, in piles of wreckage, in the grass. But mainly they are in the high, bushy hedgerows that form the fences of all the Norman fields and line every roadside and lane.

It is perfect sniping country. A man can hide himself in the thick fence-row shrubbery with several days' rations, and it's like hunting a needle in a haystack to find him.

Every mile we advance there are dozens of snipers left behind us. They pick off our soldiers one by one as they walk down the roads or across the fields.

It isn't safe to move into a new bivouac area until the snipers have been cleaned out. The first bivouac I moved into had shots ringing through it for a full day before all the hidden

---

8. In Tunisia.
9. Monte Cassino in Italy.

gunmen were rounded up. It gives you the same spooky feeling that you get on moving into a place you suspect of being sown with mines.

In past campaigns our soldiers would talk about the occasional snipers with contempt and disgust. But here sniping has become more important, and taking precautions against it is something we have had to learn and learn fast.

One officer friend of mine said, 'Individual soldiers have been sniper-wise before, but now we're sniper-conscious as whole units.'

Snipers kill as many Americans as they can, and then when their food and ammunition run out, they surrender. To an American, that isn't quite ethical. The average American soldier has little feeling against the average German soldier who has fought an open fight and lost. But his feelings about the sneaking snipers can't very well be put into print. He is learning how to kill the snipers before the time comes for them to surrender.

As a matter of fact, this part of France is very difficult for anything but fighting between small groups. It is a country of little fields, every one bordered by a thick hedge and a high fence of trees. There is hardly any place where you can see beyond the field ahead of you. Most of the time a soldier doesn't see more than a hundred yards in any direction.

In other places the ground is flooded and swampy with a growth of high, jungle-like grass. In this kind of stuff, it is almost man-to-man warfare. One officer who has served a long time in the Pacific says this fighting is the nearest thing to Guadalcanal that he has seen since.

***

Thousands of little personal stories will dribble out of D-Day on the Normandy beachhead. A few that I pick up from time to time I will pass along to you.

The freakiest story I've heard is of an officer who was shot through the face. He had his mouth wide open at the time, yelling at somebody. The bullet went in one cheek and right through his mouth without touching a thing not even his teeth, and out the other cheek. That sounds dreadful, but actually, the wound is a fairly slight one and the officer will be in action again before very long.

***

Capt. Ralph L. Haga, of Prospect, Va. claims the distinction of being the first American chaplain to set foot on French soil in World War II. He hit the beach 65 minutes after H-Hour, with the combat engineer unit to which he is attached. Like everybody else, he had rough going, but he wasn't hurt. He is a Methodist, and before the war was a pastor at Bassett, Va.

6/27/44
On the Cherbourg Peninsula

For a couple of days, I rode around the Cherbourg Peninsula with Bert Brandt, war photographer for Acme Newspictures. You may have seen by now some of the pictures Bert took during that time, so I would like to tell you how they came about.

Barneville, 18th June: the Mayor, wearing the traditional French beret, is walking towards a soldier from the 9th Infantry Division, before a crowd of villagers.
© *Photo Bert Brandt/National Archives USA*

Picture No. 1: This showed a large crowd of French people, led by the mayor of their town, advancing toward an American soldier with outstretched hands of welcome.

Well, that was taken in Barneville. The people really did welcome us, but, of course, the actual picture had to be staged.

The people were very pleased and eager. The soldier Bert picked out to receive the throng was Sergt. Max Monsorno, of (9817 96th St.) Woodhaven, Long Island. He was one of the Ninth Division men left to guard the town after the others had passed on through.

Bert instructed the crowd in its act, through the only Barneville woman who spoke English. She told them how they should advance toward the sergeant, all smiling, and be sure to look at the Sergeant and not at the camera. Then Bert yelled, 'Go!' The mayor walked toward Sergeant Monsorno with his hand out. The crowd surged up behind him, Bert snapped a picture, and then shouted at them to do it again. It seemed the mayor wasn't smiling big enough to suit Bert.

More instructions. More interpretations. A little girl jumped up and down with delight. The older people got more excited. Sergeant Monsorno gave the mayor a colossal stage smile, to show him how.

Then Bert yelled, 'Go!' again, the mayor almost cut his head in two with his smile, and the little girls threw their flowers, and the whole crowd waved their arms. Everybody was very happy including Bert. And we hope we made you very happy too.

***

On the Bricquebec/Barneville road (via Valdécie), a German column taken by surprise by the American artillery. © *Photo Bert Brandt/All Rights Reserved*

Picture No. 2: Dead horses and wrecked German vehicles along the roadside. The circumstances were these:

We had caught the Germans trying to retreat down the road from Bricquebec to Barneville and plastered them with artillery. The devastation along that road was immense.

The Germans were moving with many horse-drawn vehicles as well as trucks. They were in two-wheeled French work carts, in fancy passenger buggies, in light wagons along the style of our own Wild West covered wagons.

At spots the wreckage was piled so high that traffic couldn't get through until our own engineers dragged the debris off the road. Hundreds of carts and guns and dead horses littered the road, German bodies lay sprawling, big holes pockmarked the macadam, burned out trucks lay dead by the roadsides, masses of broken and entwining telephone wire snarled the highway. That was the scene when Bert Brandt took Picture No. 2.

The picture was of a bulldozer methodically pushing dead horses and spattered trucks, all in the same scoopful, off the road into an orchard. The dozer driver went after his job with a grim got-to-do-it look on his face.

There were scores of pitifully dead horses within a space of a few yards. Some of them lay as if asleep. Others were in distorted, gnarled positions, their leg bones cracked and broken as the

bulldozer pushed. A little bunch of French people stood looking on.

Bert took his pictures while standing on the hood of a command car in which we had been riding. I sat in the back seat calling to him to hurry up and finish. Of all the war I've seen, that is the sight which has come the nearest to making me sick at the stomach.

***

With the children of Cotentin. © *Photo Indiana State Museum*

Picture No. 3: Two sweet little French girls about six years old throwing flowers to me as we passed them in our car. The circumstances:

We were on our way back to camp after taking the picture of the horses. We passed through a concrete road block the Germans had built just north of Bricquebec, as we passed through two little girls standing on top threw some flowers to us, but they missed, and the flowers fell in the road behind us.

We had gone about fifty yards when Bert said, 'Say, that would make a picture. Let's go back and get it.'

So, we backed up, got out, and indicated, largely by sign language, that we wanted the little girls to do it again. They were smart as whips. They got the idea instantly. Furthermore, they were two of the prettiest little girls you ever saw in your life.

We picked some more flowers for them. Then Bert got set in the road ahead. I got in the back seat. Bert had me put my goggles back over my eyes so that it would look as if we were going fast, although we were actually barely moving for the picture.

We had to retake the picture three times. The little girls, in their eagerness, would throw the flowers too soon. Finally, I acted as director and, as the car approached, I kept saying, 'No, no, no,' and then I remembered the French word, 'maintenant', which means 'now', and so at the right moment I called out, 'maintenant!' and they threw flowers and everything was perfect.

Then I got out of my car, and I had no sooner hit the ground then I was attacked by my two little friends, plus half a dozen more who had arrived and who had been watching, and they were all over me like a swarm of bees, laughing and kissing and hugging me till I was almost smothered.

It was completely impulsive, and I don't think it had anything to do with the 'liberation' or the war. I think it was motivated by the simple fundamental that the French like to kiss people. They don't even care who they kiss. Vive la France!

6/28/44
On the Cherbourg Peninsula

Just a column of little items.

The other day a friend and I were in a mid-peninsula town not many miles front Cherbourg and we stopped to ask a couple of young French policemen wearing dark blue uniforms and Sam Browne belts where to go to buy a certain article.

Being quite hospitable, they jumped in the car and went along to show us. After we had finished our buying, we all got back in the car. We tried to ask the policemen where they were going. They in turn asked us where we were going.

Knowing it was hopeless in our limited French to explain that we were going to our camp up the road, we merely said Cherbourg, meaning our camp was in that direction.

But the Frenchmen thought we meant to drive right into Cherbourg, which was still in German hands. Quick as a flash they jumped up, hit the driver on the shoulder to get the car stopped, shook hands rapidly all around, saluted and scurried out with a terrified, 'Au revoir.' None of that Cherbourg stuff for those boys.

***

Some of the German officers are pleased at being captured, but your died-in-the-wool Nazi is not. They brought in a young one the other day who was furious. He considered it thoroughly unethical that we fought so hard.

The Americans had attacked all night and the Germans don't like night attacks. When this special fellow was brought in he protested in rage.

'You Americans! The way you fight! This is not war! This is madness!'

The German was so outraged he never even got the irony of his own remarks - that madness though it be, it works.

Another high-ranking officer was brought in and the first thing he asked was the whereabouts of his personal orderly. When told that his orderly was deader than a mackerel, he flew off the handle and accused us of depriving him of his personal comfort.

'Who's going to dig my foxhole for me?' he demanded.

***

You remember that in the early days of the invasion a whole bevy of high-ranking Allied officers came to visit us. Generals Marshall, Eisenhower and Arnold, Admirals King and Ramsey - there was so much brass you just bumped two-star generals without even begging pardon.

Now generals, it seems, like to be brave. Or I should say that, being generals, they know they must appear to be brave in order to set an example. Consequently, a high-ranking general never ducks or bats an eye when a shell hits near him.

Well, the military police charged with conducting this glittering array of generals around our beachhead tried to get them to ride in armored cars, since the country was still full of snipers.

But, being generals, they said no, certainly not, no armored cars for us, we'll just go in open command cars like anybody else. And that's the way they did go.

But what the generals didn't know was this: taking no chances on such a collection of talent, the M.P.'s hid armored cars and tanks all along their route, behind hedges and under bushes, out of sight so that the generals couldn't see them, but there ready for action just in case anything did happen.

***

The most wrecked town I have seen so far is Saint-Sauveur-le-Vicomte, known simply as 'San Sah-Vure.' Its buildings are gutted and leaning, its streets choked with rubble, and vehicles drive over the top of it.

Bombing and shellfire from both sides did it. The place looks exactly like World War I pictures of such places as Verdun. At the edge of the town the bomb craters are so immense that you could put whole houses in them.

A veteran of the last war pretty well summed up the two wars the other day when he said,

'This is just like the last war, only the holes are bigger.'

***

So far as I know, we have entered France without anybody making a historic remark about it. Last time, you know, it was , 'Lafayette, we are here.'

The nearest I have heard to a historic remark was made by an ack-ack gunner, sitting on a mound of earth about two weeks after D-day, reading *The Stars and Stripes* from London. All of a sudden, he said'

'Say, where's this Normandy beachhead it talks about in here?'

I looked at him closely and saw that he was serious, so I said,

'Why, you're sitting on it.'

And he said,

'Well, I'll be damned. I never knowed that.'

6/29/44
On the Cherbourg Peninsula

All the American soldiers here are impressed by the loveliness of the Normandy country. Except for swampy places it is almost a dreamland of beauty. Everything is so green and rich and natural looking.

There are no fences as such. All the little fields are bordered either by high trees or by earthen ridges built up about waist-high and now after many centuries completely covered with grass, shrubbery, ferns and flowers.

Normandy differs from the English landscape mainly in that rural England is fastidiously trimmed and cropped like a Venetian garden, while in Normandy the grass needs cutting and the hedgerows are wild and everything has less of neatness and more of the way nature makes it.

The main roads in Normandy are macadam and the side roads gravel. The roads are winding, narrow, and difficult for heavy military traffic. In many places, we've made roads one-way for miles at a stretch.

The average American finds the climate of Normandy abominable, even in June. We have about one nice day for three bad days. On nice days the sky is clear blue and the sun is out and everything seems wonderful except that there is still a hidden chill in the air, and, even in your tent or under a shade tree, you're cold.

And on the bad days the whole universe is dark and you need lights in your tent at noontime and it drizzles or sprinkles, and often a cold wind blows, and your bones and your heart, too, are miserable.

Most everybody has on his long underwear. I wear four sweaters in addition to my regular uniform. Overcoats were taken away from our troops before we left England and there are a lot of our boys not too warmly clad.

There is a constant dampness in the air. At night you put your clothes under your bedroll or they're wet in the morning. All this dampness makes for ruddy cheeks and green grass. But ruddy cheeks are for girls and green grass for cows, and personally I find the ordinary American is happiest when he's good and stinking hot.

It is the custom throughout our Army, as you doubtless know, for soldiers to paint names on their vehicles. They have names on airplanes, tanks, jeeps, trucks, guns and practically everything that moves. Sometimes they have girls' names, and often they are trick names such as 'Sad Sack'[10] or 'Invasion Blues' or 'Hitler's Menace'. Well, the boys have already started painting French names on their vehicles. I saw a jeep named 'Bientôt', which means 'soon', and a motorcycle named 'Char de Mort', which means 'Chariot of Death'. Pretty soon we will be seeing jeeps named 'Yvonne' and 'Ma Petite Chérie'[11].

---

10. Sad Sack *was the name of a comic strip created by Sergeant George Baker and published as from 1942 in* Yank, *the U.S. Army magazine. The comic strip described the absurdities and humiliations of the daily lives of a soldier in the U.S. Army. Sad sack is an abbreviation of the expression 'sad sack of shit', which was commonly used by the GIs during the Second World War to describe someone who is inept, incapable.*
11. 'My Little Sweetheart'.

The names of a lot of the French towns in our area are tongue twisters for our troops, so the towns quickly become known by some unanimous application of Americanese. For instance, Bricquebec is often called Bricabrac. And Isigny was first known as Insignia but has now evolved into Easy Knee, which is closer to the French pronunciation.

I heard a funny story of one of our young fighter pilots who had to bail out one day recently, high over the English Channel.

It seems the pilots carry a small bottle of brandy in their first-aid kits, for use if they are in the water a long time or have been hurt in landing.

Well, this young pilot, once he was safely out of his plane and floating down, figured he might as well drink his before he hit the water. So, he fished it out of his pocket and drained her down while still many thousands of feet in the air.

At high altitudes liquor hits you harder than at sea level. Furthermore, this kid wasn't accustomed to drinking. The combination of the two had him tighter than a goat by the time he floated down into the channel.

A destroyer had spotted him coming down, and it fished him out almost as soon as he hit the water, Even the cold plunge didn't sober him up. He was giddy and staggering around and they couldn't keep him in one spot long enough to dry him off.

The captain of the destroyer sensed what had happened, and being afraid the kid would take cold wandering around the dock, he came up and said with affected harshness,

'What the hell are you doing here? Get below where you belong.'

Whereupon the wet young lieutenant drew himself up in indignation and with all the thick-tongued haughtiness of a plastered guest who's been insulted by his host, replied,

'I assure you, I don't propose to remain where I'm not wanted.' And forthwith he jumped overboard. The destroyer had to rescue him again.

6/30/44
Normandy

One of the most vital responsibilities during these opening weeks of our war on the Continent of Europe has been the protection of our unloading beaches and ports.

For over and through them must pass, without interruption, and in great masses, our buildup of men and material in sufficient masses to roll the Germans clear back out of France.

Nothing must be allowed to interfere with that unloading. Everything we can lay our hands on is thrown into the guarding of those beaches and ports. Allied ground troops police them from the land side. Our two navies protect them from sneak attacks by sea. Our great air supremacy makes daytime air assaults rare and costly.

It is only at night that the Germans have a chance. They do keep pecking away at us with night bombers, but their main success in this so far has been in keeping us awake and making us dig our foxholes deeper.

The job of protecting the beaches at night has been given over to the anti-aircraft artillery, or ack-ack. I read recently that we have here on the beachhead the greatest concentration of anti-aircraft guns ever assembled in an equivalent space. After three solid weeks of being kept awake all night long by the guns and having to snatch your little sleep in odd moments during the daytime, that is not hard to believe.

Here on the beachhead the falling flak becomes a real menace - one of the few times I've known that to happen in this war. Every night for weeks, pieces of exploded shells have come whizzing to earth within 50 yards of my tent. Once an unexploded ack-ack shell buried itself half a stone's throw from my tent.

A good portion of our army on the beachhead now sleeps all night in foxholes, and some of the troops have swung over to the Anzio beachhead custom of building dugouts in order to be safe from falling flak.

For a long time, I have intended doing a series about the antiaircraft gunners. I am glad I never got around to it before, for here on the Normandy beachhead our ack-ack seems to have reached its peak. Figures are not permissible, but I can say that right now we have many, many ack-ack soldiers on the beachhead and that by the time everything has arrived the number will be much larger.

And that is speaking only of ack-ack men who do nothing else. In addition, there are thousands of gunners attached to divisions and other units who double in brass when planes come over and shoot at anything that passes low.

Our ack-ack is commanded by a general officer, which indicates how important it is. His hundreds of gun batteries even intercept planes before they near the beaches. The gun positions are plotted on a big wall map in his command tent, just as the battle lines are plotted by infantry units. A daily score is kept of the planes shot down - confirmed ones and probables. Just as an example of the

effectiveness of our ack-ack, one four-gun battery alone shot down 15 planes in the first two weeks.

Up to the time this is written, the Germans don't seem to have made up their minds exactly what they are trying to do in the air. They wander around all night long, usually in singles but sometimes in numbers, but they don't do a great deal of bombing. Most of them turn away at the first near burst from one of our 90 mm guns. Our ack-ack men say they think the German pilots are yellow, but having seen the quality of German fighting for nearly two years now that is hard for me to believe.

Often, they will drop flares that will light up the whole beach area, and then fail to follow through and bomb by the light of their flares. The ack-ack men say that not more than two out of ten planes that approach the beachhead ever make their bomb runs over our shipping. You are liable to get a bomb anywhere along the coastal area, for many of the Germans apparently just salvo their bombs and hightail home.

It is indeed a spectacle to watch the anti-aircraft fire when the Germans actually get over the beach area. All the machine guns on the ships lying off the beaches cut loose with their red tracer bullets, and those on shore do too. Their bullets arch in all directions and fuse into a sky-filling pattern. The lines of tracers bend and wave and seem like streams of red water from hoses. The whole thing becomes a gigantic, animated fountain of red in the black sky. And above all this are the split-second golden flashes of big gun shells as they explode high up toward the stars.

The noise is terrific. Sometimes low clouds catch the crack of these many guns and scramble them all into one gigantic roar which rolls and thunders like the blood-curdling approach of a hurricane.

Your tent walls puff from the concussion of the guns and bombs, and the earth trembles and shakes.

If you're sleeping in a foxhole, little clouds of dirt come rolling down upon you.

When the planes are really close and the guns are pounding out a mania of sound, you put on your steel helmet in bed and sometimes you drop off to sleep with it on and wake up with it on in the morning and feel very foolish.

7/1/44
Normandy

American anti-aircraft gunners began playing their important part in the Battle of Normandy right on D-Day and shortly after H-Hour.

Ordinarily you wouldn't think of the anti-aircraft coming ashore with the infantry, but a little bit of everything came ashore on that memorable day - from riflemen to press censors, from combat engineers to chaplains - and everybody had a hand in it.

The ack-ack was given a place in the very early waves because the general in command felt that the Germans would throw what air strength they had onto the beaches that day and he wanted his men there to repel it.

As it turned out, the Germans didn't use their planes at all and the ack-ack wasn't needed to protect the landings from air attack. So, like many other units, they turned themselves into infantry or artillery and helped win the battle of the beaches.

They took infantrylike casualties, too. One unit lost half of its men and guns.

When I started rounding up material for this ack-ack series, I ran onto the story of one crew of ack-ackers who had knocked out a German 88 deeply ensconced in a thick concrete emplacement - and did it with a tiny 37 mm. gun, which is somewhat akin to David slaying Goliath.

So, I hunted up this crew to see how they did it. By that time, they had moved several miles inland. I found them at the edge of a small open field far out in the country.

Their gun had been dug into the ground. Two men sat constantly in their bucket seats behind the gun, keeping watch on the sky even in the daytime. The others slept in their pup tents under the bushes, or just loafed around and brewed an occasional cup of coffee.

The commander of this gun is Sergt. Hyman Haas, of (1620 Ocean Ave.) Brooklyn. Sergeant Haas is an enthusiastic and flattering young man who was practically beside himself with delight when I showed up at their remote position, for he had read this column back in New York but hadn't supposed our trails would ever cross in an army this big. When I told him I wanted to write a little about his crew he beamed and said,

'Oh boy! Wait till Flatbush Ave. hears about this!'[12].

Their story is this.

---

12. *Flatbush Avenue is one of New York's main avenues, located in the borough of Brooklyn.*

They came ashore behind the first wave of infantry. A narrow valley leading away from the beach at that point was blocked by the German 88, which stopped everything in front of it. So, Driver Bill Hendrix, from Shreveport, La., turned their half-track around and drove the front and back into the water so the gun would be pointing in the right direction.

Then the boys poured 23 rounds into the pillbox. Some of their shells hit the small gun slits and went inside. At the end of their firing, what Germans were left came out with their hands up.

The boys were very proud of their achievement, but I was kind of amused at their modesty. One of them said,

'The credit should go to Lieutenant Gibbs, because he gave us the order to fire.'

The lieutenant is Wallace Gibbs, of RFD 2, Providence Road, Charlotte, N.C. The other members of the crew are Corp. John Jourdain, of (1466 N. Claiborne) New Orleans; Pvt. Frank Bartolomeo, of Ulevi, Pa.; Pvt. Joseph Sharpe, of Clover, SC.; Pfc. Frank Furey of (710 Union St.) Brooklyn; Corp. Austin Laurent Jr., of (1848 Gentilly Road) New Orleans, and Pvt. Raymond Bullock, of Coello, Ill.

Their gun is named 'BLIP', which represents the first letters of Brooklyn, Louisiana, Illinois and Pennsylvania where most of the crew come from.

Our ack-ack on the Normandy beachhead can be divided into three categories. First are the machine guns, both 50 caliber and 20-millimeter. Airplanes have to be fairly low for these to be effective.

The ack-ack branch has thousands of such guns, and so does every other fighting unit. When a low-flying strafer comes in everybody who has anything bigger than a rifle shoots at him, whether he is an ack-ack man or not.

The second big category of ack-ack is the Bofors, a 40 mm long-barreled gun which can fire rapidly and with great accuracy at medium altitudes.

Our ack-ack is equipped with thousands of these, and although they can't see their targets at night, they put a lot of shells into the sky anyhow.

The big gun, and the elite, of our ack-ack is the 90 mm. This is for high-altitude shooting. It is the gun which keeps most of the planes away, and which has such a high score of planes shot down. I spent two days and nights with one of these crews, and in the next two or three days I will try to tell you what life is like for them.

7/3/44
In Normandy

This ack-ack crew of mine is having its first taste of war. And after three weeks or so of it they feel that they are the best gun crew in the best battery of the best ack-ack battalion on the beachhead.

It would be close to impossible for a German bomber to pick out their position at night, yet this crew feels that the Germans have singled them out because they're so good. As far as I can learn, practically all the other gun crews feel the same way. That's what is known in military terms as good morale.

My crew consists of 13 men. Some of them operate the dials on the gun, others load and fire it, others lug the big shells from a storage pit a few feet away.

These big 90-millimeter guns usually operate in batteries, and a battery consists of four guns and the family of technicians necessary to operate the many scientific devices that control the guns.

The four guns of this particular battery are dug into the ground in a small open field, about 50 yards apart. The gunners sleep in pup tents or under half-tracks hidden under trees and camouflage nets.

The boys work all night and sleep in the daytime. They haven't dug foxholes, for the only danger is at night and they are up firing all night.

The guns require a great deal of daytime work to keep them in shape, so half of the boys sleep in the forenoon and half in the afternoon while the other half work.

Their life is rugged, but they don't see the seamiest side of the war. They stay quite a while in one place, which makes for comfort, and they are beyond enemy artillery range. Their only danger is from bombing or strafing, and that is not too great. They are so new at war that they still try to keep themselves clean. They shave and wash their clothes regularly.

Their service section has not come over yet from England, so they have to cook their own meals. They're pretty sick of this and will be glad when the service boys and the field kitchens catch up with them. They eat ten-in-one rations[13], heating them over a fire of wooden sticks sunk into a shallow hole in the ground.

The sergeant who is commander of my gun is a farm boy from Iowa, and none of the crew are past their middle 20s. Only two of the 13 are married.

They have been overseas more than six months, and like everybody else they are terribly anxious to go home. They like to think in terms of anniversaries, and much of their conversation is given to remembering what they were doing a year ago today when they were in camp back in America. They all hope they won't have to go to the Pacific when the European war is over.

My crew are a swell bunch of boys. They all work hard and they work well together. There are no gold-brickers in the crew. As in any group of a dozen men, some are talkative and some are quiet. There are no smart-alecks among them.

Only one man in the crew speaks French. That one has already made friends with the farmers nearby, and they get such stuff as eggs and butter occasionally. They have been promised some chicken, but it hasn't showed up yet.

Although the noise and concussion of their gun are terrific, they have got used to it and none of them wears cotton in his ears. They say the two best morale-boosters are *The Stars and Stripes*[14] and letters from home.

---

13. *10-in-1 rations were among the many formats issued to GIs by the U.S. Army. In a wooden chest, two boxes contained sufficient lunches and dinners to feed ten men for one day.*
14. *The American national anthem.*

My boys are very proud of their first night on the soil of France. They began firing immediately from a field not far from the beach. The snipers were still thick in the surrounding hedges, and bullets were singing around them all night. The boys like to tell over and over how the infantry all around them were crouching and crawling along while they had to stand straight up and dig their guns in.

It takes about 12 hours of good hard work to dig in the guns when they move to a new position. They dig in one gun at a time while the three others are firing. My gun is dug into a circular pit about four feet deep and 20 feet across. This has been rimmed with a parapet of sandbags and dirt, until when you stand on the floor of the pit you can just see over the top. The boys are safe down there from anything but a direct hit.

Their gun is covered in the daytime by a large camouflage net. My crew fires anywhere from 10 to 150 shells a night. In the very early days on the beachhead, they kept firing one night until they had only half a dozen shells left. But the supply has been built up now, and there is no danger of their running short again.

The first night I was with them was a slow night and they fired only nine shells. The boys were terribly disappointed. They said it would have to turn out that the night I was with them would be the quietest and also the coldest they had ever had.

So, just because of that I stayed a second night with them. And that time we fired all night long. It was indicated that we had brought down seven of the 15 planes we fired at, and the boys were elated.

7/5/44
In Normandy

The Germans are methodical in their night air attacks on our positions in Normandy, as they are in everything else. You begin to hear the faint, faraway drone of the first bomber around 11:20 every night.

Our own planes patrol above us until darkness. It gets dusk around 11, and you are suddenly aware that the skies which have been roaring all day with our own fighters and bombers are now strangely silent. Nothing is in the air.

The ack-ack gunners, who have been loafing near their pup tents or sleeping or telling stories now go to their guns. They bring blankets from the pup tents and pile them up against the wall of the gun pit, for the nights get very cold and they will wrap up during long lulls in the shooting.

The gunners merely loaf in the gun pit as the dusk deepens into darkness, waiting for the first telephone order to start shooting. They smoke a few last-minute cigarets. Once it is dark, they can't smoke except by draping blankets over themselves for blackout. They do smoke some that way during the night, but not much.

In four or five places in the wall of the circular pit, shelves have been dug and wooden shell boxes inserted to hold reserve shells. It is just like pigeonholes in a filing cabinet.

When the firing starts, two ammunition carriers bring new shells from a dump a few feet away up to the rim of the gun pit and hand them down to a carrier waiting below, who keeps the pigeonholes filled. The gun is constantly turning in the pit and there is always a pigeonhole of fresh shells right behind it.

The shells are as long as your arm and they weigh better than 40 pounds. After each salvo the empty shell case kicks out onto the floor of the pit. These lie there until there is a lull in the firing, when the boys toss them over the rim of the pit. Next morning, they are gathered up and put in boxes for eventual shipment back to America, where they are retooled for further use.

Each gun is connected by telephone to the battery command post, in a dugout. At all times one member of each gun crew has a phone to his ear. When a plane is picked up within range, the battery commander gives a telephonic order, 'Stand by!' Each gun commander shouts the order to his crew, and the boys all jump to their positions.

Everybody in the crew knows his job and does it. There is no necessity for harshness or short words on the part of the gun commander. When a plane either gets shot down or goes out of range, and there is nothing else in the vicinity, the command is given, 'Rest!' and the crews relax and squat or lie around on the floor of the pit. But they don't leave the pit.

Sometimes the rest will be for only a few seconds. Other times it may last a couple of hours. In the long lulls the gunners wrap up in blankets and sleep on the floor of the pit - all except the man at the telephone.

It is the usual German pattern to have a lull from about 2 to 4 a.m. and then get in another good batch of bombing attempts in the last hour before dawn.

The nights are very short here now- from 11 p.m. to 5 a.m. - for which everybody is grateful. It actually starts breaking a faint dawn just about 4:30, but the Germans keep roaming around the sky until real daylight comes.

Our own patrol planes hit the sky at daylight and the Germans skedaddle. In the first few days, when our patrol planes had to come all the way from England, the boys tell of mornings when they could see our planes approaching from one direction and the Germans heading for home at the opposite side of the sky.

As soon as it is broad daylight and the last 'Rest' is given, the boys crank down the barrel of their gun until it is horizontal, and then take a sight through it onto the stone turret of a nearby barn - to make sure the night's shooting hasn't moved the gun off its position. Then some of them gather up the empty shells, others get wood fires started for heating breakfast, and others raise and tie the camouflage net.

They're all through at 7 a.m., and half of the shift crawl into their pup tent beds while the other half go to work with oil, ramrod and waste cloth to clean up and readjust the gun. There will be no more shooting until darkness comes again.

7/6/44
In Normandy

It is 11:15 at night. The sky darkens into an indistinct dusk, but it is not yet fully dark. You can make out the high hedgerow surrounding our field and the seven long barrels of the other ack-ack guns of our battery poking upwards.

We all lean against the wall of our gun pit, just waiting for our night's work to start. We have plenty of time yet. The Germans won't be here for 10 or 15 minutes.

But no. Suddenly the gun commander, who is at the phone, yells, 'Stand by!'

The men jump to their positions. The plane is invisible, but you can hear the distant motors throbbing in the sky. Somehow you can always sense, just from the tempo in which things start, when it is going to be a heavy night. You feel now that this will be one.

One of the gunners turns a switch on the side of the gun, and it goes into remote control. From now on a mystic machine at the far end of the field handles the pointing of the gun, through electrical cables. It is all automatic. The long snout of the barrel begins weaving in the air and the mechanism that directs it makes a buzzing noise, The barrel goes up and down, to the right and back to the left, grinding and whining and jerking. It is like a giant cobra, maddened and with its head raised, weaving back and forth before striking.

Finally, the gun settles rigidly in one spot and the gun commander calls out,

'On target! Three rounds! Commence firing!'

The gun blasts forth with sickening force. A brief sheet of flame shoots from the muzzle. Dense, sickening smoke boils around in the gun pit. You hear the empty shell case clank to the ground.

Darkly silhouetted figures move silently, reloading. In a few seconds, the gun blasts again. And once again. The smoke is stifling now. You feel the blast sweep over you and set you back a little.

The salvo is fired. The men step back. You take your fingers from your ears. The smoke gradually clears. And now once more the gun is intently weaving about, grinding and whining and seeking for a new prey.

That's the way it is all night. You never see a thing. You only hear the thrump, thrump of motors in the sky and see the flash of guns and the streaking of red tracers far away. You never see the plane you're shooting at, unless it goes down in flames, and 'flamers' are rare.

I found out one thing by being with the ack-ack at night. And that is that you're much less nervous when you're out in the open with a gun in front of you than when you're doubled up under blankets in your tent, coiled and intent for every little change of sound, doubtful and imagining and terrified.

We shoot off and on, with 'rest' periods of only a few minutes, for a couple of hours. The Germans are busy boys tonight.

Then suddenly, a flare pops in the sky, out to sea, in front of us. Gradually the night brightens until the whole universe is alight and we can easily make each other out in the gun pit and see everything around us in the field.

Now everybody is tense and staring. We all dread flares. Planes are throbbing and droning all around in the sky above the light. Surely the Germans will go for the ships that are standing off the beach, or they may even pick out the gun batteries and come for us in the brightness.

The red tracers of the machine guns begin arching toward the flares but can't reach them. Then our own 'Stand by!' order comes, and the gun whines and swings and feels its way into the sky until it is dead on the high flare.

Yes, we are shooting at the flare. And our showering bursts of flak hit it, too.

You don't completely shoot out a flare. But you break it up into small pieces, and the light is dimmed, and the pieces come floating down more rapidly and the whole thing is over sooner.

Flares in the sky are always frightening. They strip you naked, and make you want to cower and hide and peek out from behind an elbow. You feel a great, welcome privacy when the last piece flickers to the ground and you can go back to shooting at the darkness from out of the dark.

7/7/44
In Normandy

The six hours of nighttime go swiftly for our ack-ack battery which is a blessing. Time races when you are firing. And in the long lulls between the waves of enemy planes you doze and catnap and the time sets away,

Once, during a lull long after midnight, half a dozen of the boys in our gun pit start singing softly. Their voices are excellent. Very low and sweetly, they sing in perfect harmony such songs as 'I've been working on the railroad' and 'Tipperary'.

There isn't anything forced, or dramatic, about it. It's just half a dozen young fellows singing because they like to sing - and the fact that they are in a gun pit in France shooting at people, trying to kill them, is just a circumstance.

The night grows bitterly chill. Between firings, every man drapes an army blanket around his shoulders, and sometimes up over his head, capelike. In the darkness they are just silhouettes, looking strange and foreign like Arabs.

After 2 o'clock there is a long lull. Gradually the boys wrap up in their blankets and lie down on the floor of the pit and fall asleep. Pretty soon you hear the snoring. I talk with the gun commander for a few minutes, in low tones. Then, my eyes get heavy too.

I wrap a blanket around me and sit down on the floor of the pit, leaning against the wall. The night is now as silent as a grave. Not a shot, not a movement anywhere.

My head slacks over to one side. But I can't relax enough to sleep in that position. And it is so cold. I am so sleepy I hurt, and I berate myself because I can't go to sleep like the others.

But I'm asleep all the time. For suddenly a voice shouts, 'Stand by!' - and it is as shocking as a bucket of cold water in your face. You look quickly at your watch and realize that an hour has passed. All the silent forms come frantically to life. Blankets fly. Men bump into each other.

'Commence firing!' rings out above the confusion, and immediately the great gun is blasting away, and smoke again fills the gun pit.

Sleep and rouse up. Catnap and fire. The night wears on. Sometimes a passing truck sounds exactly like a faraway plane. Frightened French dogs bark in distant barnyards.

Things are always confusing and mysterious in war. Just before dawn, an airplane draws nearer and nearer, lower and lower, yet we get no order to shoot and we wonder why. But machine guns and Bofors guns[15] for miles around go after it.

The plane comes booming on in, in a long dive. He seems to be heading right at us. We feel like ducking low in the pit. He actually crosses the end of our field less than a hundred yards

---

15. The Bofors was a 40mm anti-aircraft gun.

from us, and only two or three hundred foot up. Our hearts are pounding.

We don't know who he is or what he is doing. Our own planes are not supposed to be in the air. Yet if this is a German, why doesn't he bomb or strafe us? We never find out.

The first hint of dawn comes. Most of us are asleep again. Suddenly one of the boys calls out, 'Look: What's that?'

We stare into the faint light, and there just above us goes a great, silent, grotesque shape, floating slowly through the air. It is a ghostly sight.

Then we recognize it, and all of us feel a sense of relief. It is one of our barrage balloons which has broken loose and is drifting to earth[16]. Something snags it in the next field, and it hangs there poised above the apple trees until somebody comes and gets it long after daylight.

As fuller light comes, we start lighting cigarets in the open. The battery commander asks over the phone how, many shells were fired, and tells us our tentative score for the night is seven planes shot down. The crew is proud and pleased.

Dawn brings an imagined warmth and we throw off our blankets. Our eyes feel gravelly and our heads groggy. The blast of the gun has kicked up so much dirt that our faces are as grimy as though we had driven all night in a dust storm. The green Norman countryside is wet and glistening with dew.

Then we hear our own planes drumming in the distance. Suddenly they pop out of a cloud bank and are over us. Security for another day has come, and we surrender willingly the

---

16. To protect the landing beaches from aerial attacks, the Allies had deployed a vast fleet of barrage balloons above the sector, to dissuade German planes from approaching.

burden of protecting the beaches. The last 'Rest' is given and we put the gun away until another darkness comes.

7/8/44
In Normandy

The commander of my ack-ack crew is Sergt. Joseph Samuelson, a farm boy from Odebolt, Ia. 'Sam' is a quiet fellow with a mellow voice. His mouth is very wide, and right now his lips are chapped and cracked from the cold climate. He is conscientious and the others like him.

Two of the crew are from the same home town, Manchester, N.H.. They are Pvts. Armand Provencher and Jim Bresnahan. In fact, there are six Manchester boys in this battery, and 15 in the battalion. They all went into the Army the same day at the same place, and now they are firing within a few miles of each other in France.

Private Provencher is of French-Canadian extraction and is the only one of our crew who speaks French, so he does all the foraging. His family speaks French in their home back in the New Hampshire. I had always heard that the French-Canadian pas d'autre césure brand of French was unintelligible to real Frenchmen but Provencher says he doesn't have any trouble.

Three of the boys are from Massachussetts – Corp. Charles Malatesta, of Malden, George Salven, of Southbridge, and Pvt. Walter Covel, of Roxbury.

Covel has heavy black whiskers and it takes two razor blades to shave him. With a two-day growth he looks like a hobo and then when he cleans up you hardly recognize him. He asked if I'd say hello for him in the column to his mom and Bernie. I didn't ask who Bernie was but it probably wouldn't be hard to guess.

George Slavin is the entrepreneur of the battery. Back home he owns a drugstore, which his wife is running while he is away fighting. His wife keeps sending him stuff from the store until he has built up a miniature drugstore over here. He has such things as aspirin, lip pomade, shampoo and so on. He used to have a stock of cigars but they're all gone now. The boys say he gets more packages from home than any 15 other men in the battery.

Slaven and Malatesta are the only married men in the crew. Malatesta wanted me to tell his wife in the column that he loves her. So, since it is springtime and there's no law I know of against a man being fond of his wife, here goes.

Pvt. Bill Mallea, of Shelton, Conn., is the oracle of the group. He tells long and fascinating stories and thinks about the world situation and has a great sense of fun. He is the oldest man in the crew, although he isn't so old.

He's politically minded, and says he is going to become an alderman in Shelton after the war. He calls himself 'Honest Bill' Mallea. He is one of the ammunition carriers, and during lulls in the firing at night he curls up in an ammo dugout about 20 feet from the gun pit and sleeps on top of the shells. He sleeps so well you can hear him snoring clear over in the gun pit.

I didn't pick up much about the rest of the boys, but they are all pleasant lads who work hard and get along together. These others are Corp. Henry Omen, of Depew, N.Y. Pfc. Harold Dunlap of Poplar Bluffs, Mo., Pvt. Norman Kimmey, of Hanover, Pa., Corp. Clyde Libbey, of Lincoln, Me., Pfc. Jerry Fullington of Fremont Neb., and Corp. Bill Nelson Scotts Bluff, Neb.

Corporal Libbey is from the potato-growing country in Maine, and I told him, 'That Girl' and I stayed all night in Lincoln about seven years ago. But unfortunately, all I could remember about Lincoln was that we stayed there, so our attempts to dig up some mutual acquaintance or even a building we both remembered fell kind of flat.

On my second day with the battery, the boys asked their officers if it was all right for them to write in their letters home that I was staying with them. The officers said yes, so the boys all got out paper, and since it had turned warm for a change we sat and lay around on the grass while they wrote short letters home, using ammunition and ration boxes for writing boards. When they got through all of them had me sign their letters.

The boys say they didn't choose ack-ack but were just automatically put into it. They do like it, however, as long as they have to be in the Army. They are all over being gun-shy, and now that they have been through their opening weeks of war, they aren't even especially afraid.

Their battery commander is Capt. Julius Reiver, of Wilmington, Del. He stays up all night too, directing their firing from his dugout, where information is phoned in to him.

7/10/44
Normandy

One of the favorite generals among the war correspondents is Gen. Manton S. Eddy, commander of the Ninth Division.

We like him because he is absolutely honest with us, because he is sort of old-shoe and easy to talk with, and because we think he is a mighty good general. We have known him in Tunisia and Sicily, and now here in France.

Like his big chief Lieut. Gen. Omar Bradley, General Eddy looks more like a schoolteacher than a soldier. He is a big, tall man but he wears glasses and his eyes have a sort of squint. He talks like a Middle-Westerner, which he is. He still claims Chicago as home, although he has been an Army officer for 28 years. He was wounded in the last war. He is not glib, but he talks well and laughs easily.

In spite of being a professional soldier he despises war, and like any ordinary soul is appalled by the waste and tragedy of it. He wants to win it and get home just as badly as anybody else.

When the General is in the field, he lives in a truck that used to be a machine shop. They have fixed it up nicely for him with a bed, a desk, cabinets, and rugs. His orderly is an obliging, dark-skinned sergeant who is a native of Ecuador.

Some of his officers sleep in foxholes, but the General sleeps in his truck. One night, however, while I was with his division, it got too hot even for him. Fragments from shells bursting nearby, starting hitting the top of the truck, so he got out.

The general has a small mess in a tent separate from the rest of the division staff. This is because he has a good many visiting generals, and since they talk business while they eat, they must have some privacy.

Usually, he stays at his desk during the morning and makes a tour of regimental and battalion command posts during the afternoon. Usually, he goes to the front in an unarmed jeep, with another jeep right behind him carrying a machine gunner and a rifleman on the alert for snipers. His drivers say when they start out,

'Hold on, for the General doesn't spare the horses when he's traveling.'

He carries a portable telephone in his jeep, and if he suddenly wants to talk with any of his units he just stops along the road and plugs into one of the wires that are lying on the ground,

General Eddy especially likes to show up in places where his soldiers wouldn't expect to see him. He knows that it helps the soldiers' spirits to see their commanding general right up at the front where it is hot. So, he walks around the front with his long stride, never ducking or appearing to be concerned at all.

One day I rode around with him on one of his tours. At one command post, we were sitting on the grass under a tree, looking at maps, with a group of officers around us.

Our own artillery was banging nearby, but nothing was coming our way. Then, like a flash of lightning, here came a shell just over our heads, so low it went right through the treetops, it seemed. It didn't whine, it swished. Everybody, including full colonels, flopped over and began grabbing grass. The shell exploded in the next orchard.

General Eddy didn't move. He just said,

'Why, that was one of our shells.'

And since I had known General Eddy for quite a while, I was bold enough to say,

'General, if that was one of ours all I can say is that this is a hell of a way to run a war. We're fighting toward the north, and that shell was going due south.'

The General just laughed.

The General also likes to get up at 4 o'clock in the morning once in a while and go poking around into message centers and mess halls, giving the boys a start. It was one of these night meanderings that produced his favorite war story.

It was in Africa. They were in a new bivouac. It was raining cats and dogs, and the ground was knee-deep in mud. The tent pegs wouldn't stay in and the pup tents kept coming down. Everybody was wet and miserable. So, late at night the General started out on foot around the area, just because he felt so sorry for all the kids out there.

As he walked, he passed a soldier trying to re-drive the stake that held down the front of his pup tent. The soldier was using his steel helmet as a hammer, and he was having a bad time of it. Every now and then he would miss the stake with the helmet and would squash mud all over himself. He was cussing and fuming.

The General was using his flashlight, and when the soldier saw the light he called out,

'Hey, Bud, come and hold that light for me, will you?'

So General Eddy obediently squatted down and held the light while the soldier pounded and spattered mud, and they finally got the peg driven. Then, as they got up, the General said, 'Soldier, what's our name?'

The startled soldier gasped, leaned forward and looked closely, then blurted out,

'Goddelmighty !'

7/11/44
In Normandy

During the Cherbourg Peninsula campaign, I spent nine days with the Ninth Infantry Division – the division that cut the peninsula, and one of the three that overwhelmed the great port of Cherbourg.

The Cherbourg campaign is old stuff by now, and you are no longer particularly interested in it. But the Ninth Division has been in this war for a long time and will be in it for a long time to come. So, I would like to tell you some things about it.

The Ninth is one of our best divisions. It landed in Africa and it fought through Tunisia and Sicily. Then it went to England last fall and trained all winter for the invasion of France. It was one of the American divisions in the invasion that had previous battle experience.

Now an odd thing had happened to the Ninth while we were in the Mediterranean. For some reason which we have never fathomed, the Ninth wasn't released through censorship as early as it should have been, while other divisions were.

As a result, the Ninth got a complex that it was being slighted. They fought hard, took heavy casualties, and did a fine job generally, but nobody back home knew anything about it.

This lack of recognition definitely affected morale. Every commanding general is aware that publicity for his unit is a factor in morale. Not publicity in the manufactured sense, but a public report to the folks back home on what an outfit endures and what it accomplishes.

Your average doughfoot will go through his normal hell a lot more willingly if he knows that he is getting some credit for it and that the home folks know about it.

As a result of this neglect in the Mediterranean, the Ninth laid careful plans so that it wouldn't happen again. In the first place, a new censorship policy was arrived at, under which the identities of the divisions taking part in this campaign would be publicly released just as soon as it was definitely established that the Germans knew they were in combat.

With that big hurdle accomplished, the Ninth made sure that the correspondents themselves would feel at home with them... They set up a small public relations section, with an officer in charge, and a squad of enlisted men to move the correspondents' gear, and a truck to haul it, and three tents with cots, electric lights and tables.

Correspondents who came with the Ninth could get a meal, a place to write, a jeep for the front, or a courier to the rear - and at the time they asked for it.

Of course, in spite of all such facilities, a division has to be good in the first place if it is going to get good publicity. The Ninth is good. It performed like a beautiful machine in the Cherbourg campaign. Its previous battle experience paid off. Not only in individual fighting but in the perfect way the whole organization clicked. As I have tried to tell before, war depends a great deal more on organization than most people would over dream.

The Ninth did something in this campaign that we haven't always done in the past. It kept tenaciously on the enemy's neck. When the Germans would withdraw a little, the Ninth was right on top of them. It never gave them a chance to reassemble or get their balance.

The Ninth moved so fast it got to be funny. I was based at the division command post, and we struck our tents and moved forward six times in seven days.

That works the daylight out of the boys who take down and put up the tents. I overheard one of the boys saying, 'I'd rather be with Ringling Brothers.'[17]

Usually, a division headquarters is a fairly safe place. But with the Ninth it was different. Something was always happening. One night they had a bad shelling and lost some personnel. Every now and then snipers would pick off somebody. In all the time I was with them, we never had an uninterrupted night's sleep. Our own big guns were all around us and they would fire all night. Usually, German planes were over too, droning around in the darkness and making us tense and nervous.

One night, I was sitting in a tent with Capt. Lindsey Nelson, of Knoxville, when there was a loud explosion, then a shrill whine through the treetops over our heads. But we didn't jump or hit the dirt. Instead I said, 'I know what that is. That's the rotating band off one of our shells[18]. As an old artilleryman, I've heard lots of rotating bands. Sometimes they sound like a dog howling. There's nothing to be afraid of.'

---

17. The Ringling Brothers Circus was a travelling circus act founded in the United States in 1884 by five of the seven Ringling brothers. In 1907, the brothers acquired the Barnum circus, to become the largest travelling circus in the country.
18. A rotating band (or driving band) was comprised of metal rings crimped onto the circumferene of the shell. The band ensured the shell's airtightness when it entered the rifled part of the gun and enabled rotation to begin when it travelled through the gun, hence stabilising its trajectory.

'Sure,' said Captain Nelson, 'that's what it was, a rotating band.'

But our harmless rotating band we found a few minutes later, was a jagged, red-hot, foot-square fragment of steel from a 240 mm German shell which had landed a hundred yards away from us. It's wonderful to be a wise guy.

7/12/44
In Normandy

This war in Normandy is a war from hedgerow to hedgerow, and when we get into a town or city it is a war from street to street.

The other day I went along - quite accidentally, I assure you - with an infantry company that had been assigned to clean out a pocket in the suburbs of a city[19].

Since this episode was typical of the way an infantry company advances into a city held by the enemy, I would like to try to give you a picture of it. I can't do it in just one column, so you'll have to read this in instalments covering several days. I hope your patience holds out.

As I say, I hadn't intended to do it. I started out in the normal fashion that afternoon to go up to a battalion command post and just look around. I was traveling with Correspondent Charles Wertenbaker and Photographer Bob Capa, both of *Time* and *Life* magazines.

---

19. *The city in question is Cherbourg. The American troops had reached the outskirts of Cherbourg by 24 June 1944, to liberate the town centre on the 26th. The company Ernie Pyle mentions in this text was attached to the 9th Infantry Division, in charge of attacking the west of the town.*

Well, when we got to the C.P., we were practically at the front lines. The post was in a church that stood on a narrow street. In the courtyard across the street M.P.'s were frisking freshly taken prisoners.

I mingled among the prisoners awhile. They were still holding their hands high in the air, and you're pretty close to the front when prisoners do that. They were obviously frightened and eager to please their captors. A soldier standing beside me asked one German kid about the insignia on his cap, so the kid gave the insignia to him.

The prisoners had a rank odor about them, like silage. Some of them were Russians, and two of these had their wives with them. They had been living together right at the front. The women thought we were going to shoot their husbands and they were frantic.

That's one way the Germans keep these conscripted Russians fighting - they have thoroly sold them on the belief that we will shoot them as soon as they are captured.

We were just hanging around absorbing this stuff when a young lieutenant, in a trench coat and wearing sunglasses - altho' the day was miserably dark and chill - came up and said,

'Our company is starting in a few minutes to go up this road and clean out a strong point. It's about a half a mile from here. There are probably snipers in some of the houses along the way. Do you want to go along with us?'

I certainly didn't. Going into battle with an infantry company is not the way to live to a ripe old age. But when you are invited, what can you do?

So, I said, 'Sure.' And so did Wertenbaker and Capa. Wert never seems nervous, and Capa is notorious for his daring. Fine company for me to be keeping.

We walked until we were at the head of the column. As we walked, the young officer introduced himself. He was Lieut. Orion Shockley, of Jefferson City, Mo. I asked him how he got the odd name Orion. He said he was named after Mark Twain's brother.

Shockley was executive officer of the company. The company commander was Lieut. Lawrence McLaughlin, from Boston. One of the company officers was a replacement who had arrived just three hours previously and had never been in battle before. I noticed that he ducked sometimes at our own shells, but he was trying his best to seem calm.

The soldiers around us had a two-week growth of beard. Their clothes were worn slick and very dirty. They still wore the uncomfortable gas-impregnated clothes they had come ashore in.

The boys were tired. They had been fighting and moving constantly forward on foot for nearly three weeks without rest - sleeping out on the ground, wet most of the time, always tense, eating cold rations, seeing their friends die.

One of them came up to me and said, almost belligerently, 'Why don't you tell the folks back home what this is like? All they hear about is victories and a lot of glory stuff. They don't know that for every hundred yards we advance somebody gets killed. Why don't you tell them how tough this life is?'

I told him that was what I tried to do all the time. This fellow was pretty fed up with it all. He said he didn't see why his outfit wasn't sent home, that they had done all the fighting.

That wasn't true at all, for we have other divisions that have fought more and taken heavier casualties than this one. Exhaustion will make a man feel like that. A few days' rest usually has him smiling again.

As we waited to start our advance, the low black skies of Normandy let loose on us and we gradually became hopelessly soaked to the skin.

7/13/44
In Normandy

Lieut. Orion Shockley came over with a map and explained to us just what his company was going to do. There was a German strong point of pillboxes and machine-gun nests about half a mile down the street ahead of us.

Our troops had made wedges into the city on both sides of us, but nobody had yet been up this street where we were going. The street, they thought, was almost certainly under rifle fire.

'This is how we'll do it,' the lieutenant said. 'A rifle platoon goes first. Right behind them will go part of a heavy-weapons platoon, with machine guns to cover the first platoon. Then comes another rifle platoon. Then a small section with mortars, in case they run into something pretty heavy. Then another rifle platoon. And bringing up the rear, the rest of the heavy-weapons outfit to protect us from behind. We don't know what we'll run into, and I don't want to stick you right out in front, so why don't you come along with me? We'll go in the middle of the company.'

I said, 'Okay.' By this time, I wasn't scared. You seldom are once you're into something. Anticipation is the worst. Fortunately, this little foray came up so suddenly there wasn't time for much anticipation.

The rain kept on coming down, and you could sense that it had set in for the afternoon. None of us had raincoats, and by evening there wasn't a dry thread on any of us. I could go back to a tent for the night, but the soldiers would have to sleep the way they were.

Waiting to take a delicate step. © *Photo Robert Capa/Magnum Photos*

We were just ready to start when, all of a sudden, bullets came whipping savagely right above our heads.

'It's those damn 20 millimeters again,' the lieutenant said. 'Better hold it up a minute.'

The soldiers all crouched lower behind the wall. The vicious little shells whanged into a grassy hillside just beyond us. A

French suburban farmer was hitching up his horses in a barnyard on the hillside. He ran into the house. Shells struck all around it.

Two dead Germans and a dead American still lay in his driveway. We could see them when we moved up a few feet.

The shells stopped, and finally the order to start was given. As we left the protection of the high wall, we had to cross a little culvert right out in the open and then make a turn in the road.

The men went forward one at a time. They crouched and ran, apelike, across this dangerous space. Then, beyond the culvert, they filtered to either side of the road, stopping and squatting down every now and then to wait a few moments.

The lieutenant kept yelling at them as they started,

'Spread it out now. Do you want to draw fire on yourselves? Don't bunch up like that. Keep five yards apart. Spread it out, dammit.'

There is an almost irresistible pull to get close to somebody when you are in danger. In spite of themselves, the men would run up close to the fellow ahead for company.

The other lieutenant now called out,

'Now you on the right watch the left side of the street for snipers, and you on the left watch the right side. Cover each other that way.'

And a first sergeant said to a passing soldier,

'Get that grenade out of its case. It won't do you no good in the case. Throw the case away. That's right.'

Some of the men carried grenades already fixed in the ends of their rifles. All of them had hand grenades. Some had big

Browning automatic rifles. One carried a bazooka. Interspersed in the thin line of men every now and then was a medic with his bags of bandages and a Red Cross arm band on the left arm. The men didn't talk any. They just went.

They weren't heroic figures as they moved forward one at a time, a few seconds apart. You think of attackers as being savage and bold. These men were hesitant and cautious. They were really the hunters, but they looked like the hunted. There was a confused excitement and a grim anxiety in their faces.

They seemed terribly pathetic to me. They weren't warriors. They were American boys who by mere chance of fate had wound up with guns in their hands sneaking up a death-laden street in a strange and shattered city in a faraway country in a driving rain. They were afraid, but it was beyond their power to quit. They had no choice.

They were good boys. I talked with them all afternoon as we sneaked slowly forward along the mysterious and rubbled street, and I know they were good boys.

And even though they aren't warriors born to the kill, they win their battles. That's the point.

7/14/44
In Normandy

It was about time for me to go - out alone into that empty expanse of 15 feet - as the infantry company I was with began its move into the street that led to what we did not know.

One of the soldiers asked if I didn't have a rifle. Every time you're really in the battle lines, they'll ask you that. I said no, correspondents weren't allowed to; it was against international law. The soldiers thought that didn't seem right.

Finally, the sergeant motioned - it was my turn. I ran with bent knees, shoulders hunched, out across the culvert and across the open space. Lord, but you felt lonely out there.

I had to stop right in the middle of the open space, to keep my distance behind the man ahead. I got down behind a little bush, as though that would have stopped anything.

Just before starting, I had got into a conversation with a group of soldiers who were to go right behind me. I was just starting to put down the boys' names when my turn came to go. So, it wasn't till an hour or more later, during one of our long waits as we sat crouching against some buildings, that I worked my way back along the line and took down their names.

It was pouring rain, and as we squatted down for me to write on my knee, each soldier would have to hold my helmet over my notebook to keep it from being soaked. Here are the names of just a few of my 'company mates' in that little escapade that afternoon:

- Sergt. Joseph Palajsa, of (187 1 St.) Pittsburgh.
- Pfc. Arthur Greene, of (618 Oxford St.) Auburn, Mass. His New England accent was so broad I had to have him spell out 'Arthur' and 'Auburn' before I could catch what he said.
- Pfc. Dick Medici, of (5231 Lemy Ave.) Detroit.
- Lieut. James Giles, a platoon leader, from Athens, Tenn. He was so wet, so worn, so soldier-looking that I was startled, when he said 'lieutenant', for I thought he was a GI.

- Pfc. Arthur Slageter, of (3915 Taylor Ave,) Cincinnati. He was an old reader of this column back home, and therefore obviously a fine fellow.
- Pfc. Robert Edie, of New Philadelphia Pa. Edie is 30, he is married, and he used to work in a brewery back home. He is a bazooka man, but his bazooka was broken that day, so he was just carrying a rifle.
- Pfc. Ben Rienzi, of (430 E. 115 St.) New York.
- Sergt. Robert Hamilton, of (2940 Robbins Ave.) Philadelphia, who was wounded in Africa.
- And Sergt. Joe Netscavge, of Shenandoah, Pa., who sports two souvenirs of the Normandy campaign - a deep dent in his helmet, where a sniper's bullet glanced off, and a leather cigaret case he got from a German prisoner.

These boys were Ninth Division veterans, most of whom had fought in Tunisia and Sicily too.

Gradually we moved on, a few feet at a time. The soldiers hugged the walls on both sides of the street, crouching all the time. The city around us was still full of sound and fury. You couldn't tell where anything was coming from or going to.

The houses had not been blown down along this street. But now and then a wall would have a round hole through it, and the windows had all been knocked out by concussion and shattered glass littered the pavements. Gnarled telephone wire was lying everywhere.

It was a poor district. Most of the people had left the city. Shots, incidentally, always sound louder and distorted in the vacuumlike emptiness of a nearly deserted city. Lonely doors and shutters banged noisily back and forth.

All of a sudden, a bunch of dogs came yowling down the street, chasing each other. Apparently, their owners had left without them, and they were running wild. They made such a noise that we shooed them on in the erroneous fear that they would attract the Germans' attention.

The street was a winding one and we couldn't see as far ahead as our forward platoon. But soon we could hear rifle shots not far ahead, and the rat-tat-tat of our machine guns, and the quick blirp-blirp of German machine pistols.

For a long time, we didn't move at all. While we were waiting the lieutenant decided to go into the house we were in front of. A middle-aged Frenchman and his wife were in the kitchen. They were poor people.

The woman was holding a terrier dog in her arms, belly up, the way you cuddle a baby, and soothing it by rubbing her cheek against its head. The dog was trembling with fear from the noise.

Pretty soon the word was passed back down the line that the street had been cleared as far as a German hospital[20] about a quarter of a mile ahead. There were lots of our own wounded in that hospital and they were now being liberated.

So, Lieutenant Shockley and Wertenbaker and Capa and myself got up and went up the street, still keeping close to the walls. I lost the others before I had gone far. For, as I would pass doorways soldiers would call out to me and I would duck in and talk for a moment and put down a name or two.

By now, the boys along the line were feeling cheerier, for no word of casualties had been passed back. And, up here, the

---

20. *The Navy hospital located at the western entrance to Cherbourg.*

city was built up enough so that the waiting riflemen had the protection of doorways. It took me half an hour to work my way up to the hospital - and then the excitement began.

7/15/44
In Normandy

The hospital was in our hands, but just barely. On up the street a block, there seemed to be fighting. I say seemed to be, because actually, you can't always tell. Street fighting is just as confusing as field fighting.

One side will bang away for a while then the other side. Between these sallies there are long lulls, with only stray and isolated shots. Just an occasional soldier is sneaking about, and you don't see anything of the enemy at all. You can't tell half the time just what the situation is, and neither can the soldiers.

About a block beyond the hospital entrance, two American tanks were sitting in the middle of the street, one about 50 yards ahead of the other. I walked toward them. Our infantrymen were in doorways along the street.

I got within about 50 feet of our front tank when it let go its 75-millimeter gun. The blast was terrific there in the narrow street. Glass came tinkling down from nearby windows, smoke puffed around the tank, and the empty street was shaking and trembling with the concussion.

As the tank continued to shoot, I ducked into a doorway, because I figured the Germans would shoot back. Inside the doorway there was a sort of street-level cellar, dirt-floored. Apparently, there was a wine shop above, for the cellar was stacked with wire crates for holding wine bottles on their sides. There were lots of bottles, but they were all empty.

I went back to the doorway and stood peeking out at the tank. It started backing up. Then suddenly, a yellow flame pierced the bottom of the tank and there was a crash of such intensity that I automatically blinked my eyes. The tank, hardly 50 feet from where I was standing, had been hit by an enemy shell.

A second shot ripped the pavement at the side of the tank. There was smoke all around, but the tank didn't catch fire. In a moment, the crew came boiling out of the turret.

Grim as it was, I almost had to laugh as they ran toward us. I have never seen men run so violently. They ran all over, with arms and heads going up and down and with marathon-race grimaces. They plunged into my doorway.

I spent the next excited hour with them. We changed to another doorway and sat on boxes in the empty hallway. The floor and steps were thick with blood where a soldier had been treated within the hour.

What had happened to the tank was this. They had been firing away at a pillbox ahead when their 75 backfired, filling the tank with smoke and blinding them.

They decided to back up in order to get their bearings, but after backing a few yards, the driver was so blinded that he stopped. Unfortunately, he stopped exactly at the foot of a side street. More

unfortunately, there was another German pillbox up the side street. All the Germans had to do was take easy aim and let go at the sitting duck.

The first shot hit a tread, so the tank couldn't move. That was when the boys got out. I don't know why the Germans didn't fire at them as they poured out.

The escaped tankers naturally were excited, but they were as jubilant as June-bugs and ready for more. They had never been in combat before the invasion of Normandy, yet in three weeks their tank had been shot up three times. Each time it was repaired and put back in action. And it can be repaired again this time. The name of their tank, appropriately, is 'Be Back Soon.'

The main worry of these boys was the fact that they had left the engine running. We could hear it chugging away. It's bad for a tank motor to idle very long. But now they were afraid to go back and turn the motor off, for the tank was still right in line with the hidden German gun.

Also, they had come out wearing their leather crash helmets. Their steel helmets were still inside the tank, and so were their rifles. 'We'll be a lot of good without helmets or rifles!' one of them said.

The crew consisted of Corp. Martin Kennelly, of (8040 Langley St.) Chicago, the tank commander; Sergt. L. Wortham, Leeds, Ala., driver; Pvt. Ralph Ogren, of (3551 32nd Ave. South) Minneapolis, assistant driver; Corp. Albin Stoops, Marshalltown, Del., gunner, and Pvt. Charles Rains, of (1317 Madison St.) Kansas City, the loader.

Private Rains was the oldest of the bunch, and the only married one. He used to work as a guard at the Sears, Roebuck[21] plant in Kansas City.

'I was M.P.[22] to 1,500 women,' he said with a grin, 'and how I'd like to be back doing that!' The other tankers all expressed loud approval of this sentiment.

7/17/44
In Normandy

Tank Commander Martin Kennelly of Chicago wanted to show me just where his tank had been hit. As a matter of fact, he hadn't seen it for himself yet, for he came running up the street the moment he jumped out of the tank,

So, when the firing died down a little, we sneaked up the street until we were almost even with the disabled tank. But we were careful not to get our heads around the corner of the side street, for that was where the Germans had fired from.

The first shell had hit the heavy steel brace that the tread runs on, and then plunged on through the side of the tank, very low. 'Say!' Kennelly said in amazement. 'It went right through our

lower ammunition storage box: I don't know what kept the ammunition from going off. We'd have been a mess if it had. Boy, it sure would have got hot in there in a hurry!'

---

21. *Sears, Robuck and Company was a chain with stores in all major American cities, but also in country locations, up to the end of the Second World War. At the time, it was the very first company of its kind in the United States.*
22. *Military Police.*

The street was still empty. Beyond the tank about two blocks was a German truck, sitting all alone in the middle of the street. It had been blown up, and its tires had burned off. This truck was the

only thing you could see. There wasn't a human being in sight anywhere.

Then an American soldier came running up the street shouting for somebody to send up a medic. He said a man was badly wounded just ahead. He was extremely excited, yelling, and getting madder because there was no medic in sight.

Word was passed down the line and, pretty soon, a medic came out of a doorway and started up the street. The excited soldier yelled at him and began cussing, and the medic broke into a run. They ran past the tanks together, and up the street a way they ducked into a doorway.

On the corner just across the street from where we were standing was a smashed pillbox. It was in a cut-away corner like the entrances to some of our corner drugstores at home, except that instead of there being a door, there was a pillbox of reinforced concrete, with gun slits.

The tank boys had shot it to extinction and then moved their tank up even with it to get the range of the next pillbox. That one was about a block ahead, set in a niche in the wall of a building. That's what the boys had been shooting at when their tank was hit. They knocked it out, however, before being knocked out themselves.

For an hour there was a lull in the fighting. Nobody did anything about a third pillbox, around the corner. Our second tank pulled back a little and just waited. Infantrymen worked their way up to second-story windows and fired their rifles up the side street without actually seeing anything to shoot at.

Now and then, blasts from a 20 mm gun would splatter the buildings around us. Then, our second tank would blast back in that general direction, over the low roofs, with its machine gun. There was a lot of dangerous-sounding noise, but I don't think anybody on either side got hit.

Then we saw coming up the street, past the wrecked German truck I spoke of, a group of German soldiers. An officer walked in front, carrying a Red Cross flag on a stick. Bob Capa, the photographer, braved the dangerous funnel at the end of the side street where the damaged tank stood, leap-frogging past it and on down the street to meet the Germans.

At the crossroads between Rue Pierre-de-Coubertin and Rue Lelédier in Cherbourg (on the left, you can see the palisade around the public stadium). © *Photo Robert Capa/Magnum Photos*

First, he snapped some pictures of them. Then, since he speaks German, he led them on back to our side of the invisible fence of battle. Eight of them were carrying two litters bearing two wounded German soldiers. The others walked behind with their hands up. They went on past us to the hospital. We assumed that they were from the second knocked-out pillbox.

I didn't stay to see how the remaining pillbox was knocked out. But I suppose our second tank eventually pulled up to the corner, turned, and let the pillbox have it. After that, the area would be clear of everything but snipers.

The infantry, who up till then had been forced to keep in doorways, would now continue up the street and poke into the side streets and into the houses until everything was clear.

That's how a strong point in a city is taken. At least that's how ours was taken. You don't always have tanks to help, and you don't always do it with so little shedding of blood.

But the city was already crumbling when we started in on this strong point, which was one of the last, and they didn't hold on too bitterly. But we didn't know that when we started.

I hope this has given you a faint idea of what street fighting is like. If you got out of it much more than a headful of confusion then, you've got out of it exactly the same thing as the soldiers who do it.

7/18/44
In Normandy

One day while we were up on the Cherbourg peninsula, I decided all of a sudden that I couldn't face C-rations that evening. And Bob Capa, the photographer, said he never could face C-rations in the first place[23]. So, we laid a plan.

We got a friendly mess sergeant to drum us up some cans of Vienna sausage, some sugar, canned peas, and what not, and we put them in a pasteboard box.

Ernie Pyle posing with his colleague, the photographer Bert Brandt, in the town hall square in Cherbourg. The photograph must have been taken shortly after the town was liberated on 26th June. © *Photo Indiana State Museum*

---

23. In the U.S. Army, C rations were canned food rations that had not been prepared in kitchens. A rations were those made from fresh produce and B rations were prepared.

Then we walked around a couple of hedgerows to our motor pool and dug out Pvt. Lawrence Wedley Cogan from the comfortable lair he had prepared for himself in an oats field.

Private Cogan drives a command car for the G-2 section of the Ninth Infantry Division. When we can catch him, not driving for G-2, we can talk him into driving us somewhere.

So, we piled in and directed Chauffeur Cogan to set out for the nearby village of Les Pieux. When we got there, Capa, who speaks eight languages - and as his friends say, 'none of them well' - went into a restaurant to make his investigations.

Pretty soon he came to the door and motioned. So, Cogan parked the car behind a building, we took our box of canned stuff, and in we went.

It was a typical French village restaurant, with low ceilings, and floors that sagged, and it consisted of four or five rooms. It was crammed with French people, for we had only just taken Les Pieux and not many Americans had found the place yet.

The woman who ran the place took us to a long table. Private Cogan was dirty with the grease and dust of his job and went off to wash before eating again in civilized fashion.

The cosmopolitan Capa made a deal and we traded our rations for the cafe's regular dinner, in order not to take anything away from the French. We had expected to pay the full price anyhow, but when the bill came, they charged us only for the cooking, and wouldn't take a bit more.

The restaurant had no small tables, but one long one in each room. Consequently, we were seated with French people. They seemed eager to be friendly, and pretty soon we were in the thick of conversation. That is, Capa and the French were in conversation, and occasionally, he would relay the gist of it to Cogan and me, the hicks.

The people told us about the German occupation, but they didn't have much bad to say about the Germans. Then we talked of the French underground which had just been coming out in the open in the previous few days.

Throughout our dinner Private Cogan, in his soiled coveralls, listened and beamed and ate and took in eagerly the words he couldn't understand and the scene so new and strange to him.

One middle-aged Frenchwoman made over him because he looked so young. Cogan isn't bashful, but he couldn't talk French so he just grinned. Private Cogan joined the Army at 17. He was overseas before he was 18, and he is only 19 now. His home is at (128 E. Walnut St.) Alexandria, Va. He is one of the nicest human beings you ever met.

No matter what you ask him to do, or what time of night it is, or in what weather you dig him out, he does it goodnaturedly and without the silent surliness of some drivers. Furthermore, he is an excellent driver, and he always has a box of rations in his car,

When we left the restaurant, he was all a-bubble and said over and over again that he'd had the best time that evening he had ever had in the Army. Imagine him, he said, seeing foreign stuff like this as young as he is.

Next day the international trio, Capa, Cogan and Pyle, went out again. But this time it was different. This was the trip I've been writing about the past several days, when we went into

Cherbourg with an attacking infantry company of the Ninth Division.

When we got to our forward battalion command post, we got out of the car and told Cogan to go back about a mile and wait for us, as it was too dangerous to wait up there. And do you know what Cogan did? Cogan looked at us almost pleadingly, and said,

'Would you let me go with you?'

We said of course, if he wanted to, Cogan jumped out of the car like a jumpingjack, buckled on two big belts of ammunition, grabbed his rifle, and was ready to go.

He stayed with us clear through that afternoon. When Capa went farthest forward to get his pictures of surrendering Germans, Cogan hopped along behind him with his loaded rifle, as though to protect him. Now and then I would notice his face, and instead of being afraid he was as pleased as a child at a state fair.

Of course, what he did will seem asinine to any combat soldier who would give a fortune to keep out of combat instead of seeking it. Yet the willingness to do anything that is asked of you, and the eagerness to experience things that aren't asked of you, make a real trooper.

When we got to camp that night Capa said,

'That Cogan, he's one of the finest soldiers I've ever met in this Army.' Righto.

7/19/44
In Normandy

Everything seems odd in Normandy. The hedgerows are thick and ancient. The stone walls are sometimes so mounded over with earth that you don't know there's a wall beneath. The trees in the apple orchards are mellow with moss so thick that it seems like a coat of green velvet.

The towns and cities are just as old and worn-looking. I have yet to see a building in Normandy that appeared to have been built within the last three generations.

The tone is not one of decadence, but just of great and content age. Even Cherbourg was a surprise. All of its buildings were old and worn.

It was a contrast to other war cities we have passed through - Algiers and Palermo and even Naples - where much building and remodeling have been done in this century, and the new homes are shiny and modernistic, and the street fronts look almost American.

A street scene in Cherbourg looks so much like the Hollywood sets of old European cities that you get your perspective reversed and feel that Cherbourg has just been copied from a movie set.

It's the same way with the Norman architecture. The houses aren't so smooth and regular and nice as California homes of Norman design. When you look at them you feel, before catching yourself, that they have copied our California Norman homes and not done too good a job.

Everything is of stone. Even the barns and cowsheds are stone - and in exactly the same design and usually the same size as the houses. They are grouped closely together around a square, so that a farmer's home makes a compact little settlement of buildings that resembles a country estate at a distance.

Normandy is dairy country. Right now, the people have more butter on their hands than they know what to do with. It is a stupid soldier indeed who can't get himself all the butter he wants. But even though it is a glut on the market, the French still ask 60 cents a pound for it.

When the Germans were here, they bought all the Norman butter, and at fancy prices too. German soldiers would ship it home to their families. And although their New Order is strict and full of promises of ordered world, the Germans themselves created and fostered the Paris black market, according to the local people.

Much of the butter bought in Normandy by German officers went to Paris for resale at unheard-of prices.

To be honest about it, we can't sense that Normandy suffered too much under the German Occupation. That is no doubt less because of German beneficence than because of the nature of the country. For in any throttled country, the farm people always come out best.

Normandy is rich agriculturally. The people can sustain themselves. It is in the cities that occupation hurts worst. I suspect that when we get to Paris, we will hear an entirely different story from the people.

Normandy is certainly a land of children. It seems to me there are more children here even than in Italy. And I'll have to break down and admit one thing: they are the most beautiful children I have ever seen.

It is an exception when you see a child who isn't exceptionally good-looking. Apparently, they grow out of this, however, for on the whole the Norman adults look like people anywhere - both good and bad. One thing about the Normans is in contrast with the temperament we have known so long in the Mediterranean. The people here are hard workers. Some of the American camps and city offices hire teen-age French boys for kitchen and office work, and I've noticed that they go at their work eagerly and like the wind.

The story of the French underground, when the day comes for it to be written, will be one of the most fascinating things in all history.

On the Cherbourg peninsula, the underground was made up of cells, five people to a cell. Those five know each other, but none of them knew any other members of the underground anywhere.

It was fun to see the Frenchmen on the day the underground began coming out into the open. They identified themselves by special arm bands that they had kept in hiding. One underground man would look at a neighbor wearing an arm-band and exclaim in amazement,

'What! You too?'

In one village we asked some people who were not in the movement if they had ever known who the underground members in their town were. They said they could pretty well guess, just from the character of the people but never actually knew for sure.

7/20/44
In Normandy

Capt. John Jackson is an unusual fellow with an unusual job. It has fallen to his lot to be the guy who goes in and brings out German generals who think maybe they would like to surrender.

This happens because he speaks German, and because he is on the staff of the Ninth. Division, which captured the German generals commanding the Cherbourg area.

Captain Jackson goes by the nickname of 'Brinck'. He is a bachelor, 32 years old. It is quite a coincidence that he was born in the town of Dinard, about 30 miles from Cherbourg[24]. But he is straight American, for generations back. His folks just happened to be traveling over here at the time he showed up.

Captain Jackson's mother lives in New Canaan, Conn., but he likes to think of New Mexico as home. For several years he has been a rancher out there and he loves it. His place is near Wagon Mound and Klines Corners, about 40 miles east of Santa Fe. The war has played hob with his business. Both he and his partner are overseas, and there's nobody left to look after the business. They lost money last year for the first time.

---

24. Ernie Pyle's estimation of distances and knowledge of French geography were somewhat approximative. From Dinard to Cherbourg, there is a distance of around 220 kilometres (136 miles).

No clues on the site of this photograph. Perhaps the American press correspondents' camp in Vouilly? All we know is that it was taken on 20 July 1944 by Bert Brandt. © *Photo Indiana State Museum*

Captain Jackson is a short, dark man with a thin face. He wears a long trench coat with pack harness[25], and his helmet comes down over his ears, giving him the appearance of a Russian soldier rather than American.

He speaks perfect French, but he says his German is only so-so. He says it is actually better in his job not to speak flawless German, for then the German officers would think he was a German turned American and would be so contemptuous they wouldn't talk to him.

Another remarkable character is Pfc. Ivan Sanders. Sanders is the 'Mister Fixit' of the Ninth Division. His actual job is that of electrician, but his native knack for fixing things has led him into a sort of haloed status that keeps him working like a dog 24 hours a day, doing things for other people.

No matter what gets out of fix, Sanders can fix it. Without previous experience, he now repairs fountain pans, radios, electric razors, typewriters, broken knives, stoves and watches. He has become an institution. Everybody from the commanding general on down depends on him and yells for him whenever anything goes wrong. There is just one thing about Sanders. Nobody can get him to clean up. He is a sight to behold.

Even the commanding general just threw up his hands about a year ago and gave up. When distinguished visitors come, they try to hide Sanders. But the funny part about Sanders's deplorable condition is that he is eager to be clean. They just never give him time to wash. They keep him too busy fixing things.

---

25. Set of belts and straps worn by soldiers on their chests and around their waists and enabling them to attach their flask, cartridge belts, map holders, etc.

In civil life Sanders was an auto mechanic. He comes from Vinton, Ia. After the war, he guesses he will set up another auto repair shop. He figures there will be enough veterans with cars to keep him busy.

Another unusual thing about Sanders is that he doesn't have to be over here at all. He is 43, and he has had three chances to go home. And do you know why he turned them down? It's because he's so conscientious, he figures they couldn't get anybody else to do his work properly!

***

Small-world stuff:

One evening I dropped past an ack-ack battery I know, and a Red Cross man who served in this brigade came over and introduced himself.

He did look vaguely familiar, but I couldn't have told you who he was. And no wonder - it had been 21 years since I'd seen him.

His name was Byron Wallace. He was a freshman at Indiana University when I was a senior. He belonged to the Delta Upsilon fraternity and lived just across the alley from us. His hometown was at Washington, Ind.

Ever since college, he has been in recreational and physical education work - in New York's Bowery, in Los Angeles, in Pittsburgh. And now in Normandy. He came ashore on D-plus-one. He thinks he's going to like it here all right.

7/21/44
In Normandy

In front of General Manton Eddy, commander of the U.S. 9th Infantry Division, the German General von Schlieben, commander of the Fortress of Cherbourg, is photographed shortly after surrendering the town. © *Photo Robert Capa/Magnum Photos*

When the now famous general, Carl Wilhelm von Schlieben[26], was captured it happened to be at the Ninth Division command post to which he was first brought. Major General Manton S. Eddy, division commander, had a long interview with him in his trailer. When he was about finished and ready to send the captured general on to higher headquarters, General Eddy sent word that the photographers could come and take pictures. So they stood in a group in an orchard while the photographers snapped away. Von Schlieben was obviously sourpuss about being captured, and even more sourpuss at having his picture taken. He made no effort to look other than sullenly displeased.

General Eddy was trying to be decent about it. He had an interpreter tell the prisoner that this was the price of being a general. Von Schlieben just snorted. And then General Eddy said to the interpreter, 'Tell the general that our country is a democracy and therefore I haven't the authority to forbid these photographers to take pictures.'

Von Schlieben snorted again. And we chuckled behind our beards at one of the slickest examples of working democracy we had ever seen. And General Eddy had the appearance of the traditional cat that swallowed something wonderful.

***

Normandy is a land of rabbits. We saw them in the fields and around the farmyards. Most of them were semi-tame. Apparently, the people eat a great deal of rabbit. When we first moved in and began capturing permanent German bivouac

---

26. *General von Schlieben was in command of the Fortress of Cherbourg. He was captured by the Americains on 26 June 1944.*

areas, we found that nearly every little group of German soldiers had its own rabbit warren. They raised them for food.

One day my friend Private William Bates Wescott found a mother rabbit that had been killed in the shelling and, nearby, in a nest under a hedge, he found six baby rabbits, only a few days old. Wescott took them to his pup tent, got a ration box to put them in, and spent the afternoon feeding them condensed milk through an eye-dropper. They went for it like little babies. Next morning five of them were dead. The soldiers said the concussion of bombs falling during the night had killed them. I said undiluted condensed milk had killed them. At any rate, the sixth one thrived and became cute and gay. He followed Wescott around everywhere, and if the distance got too far, he would go hopping back to the pup tent and snuggle up in Wescott's blankets. He was quite a little rabbit. Everybody was crazy about him. Then after about a week we found him dead out on the grass one morning. Which is a lousy way to end the story, but that's all there was to it.

***

The town of Montebourg on the Cherbourg peninsula was one of the worst-wrecked towns, shelled by both sides. We stopped at Montebourg the day after it was all over[27]. On one side of the city square there was a large collection of rusting farm implements - all kinds of plows, planters, mowers and things. On one wrecked mowing machine was the familiar name 'McCormick'. And near the machine was stretched out in pathetic death a big white rabbit.

***

---

27. *Montebourg was permanently liberated by the U.S. troops on 19 June 1944. The town had been subjected to constant bombardments since the 6th of June.*

One night I crawled down into an ack-ack battery command post, in a dugout. It was about 2 a.m. Only two people were there - a lieutenant, giving orders to the guns by telephone, and a sergeant, getting ready to fix some hot chocolate. He asked if I would have some and, following the old Army custom of never refusing anything, I said sure.

He was Sergeant Leopold Lamparty, first sergeant of the battery, from 916 Franklin Street, Youngstown, Ohio. He used to be a bartender, and in France he had already picked up several little antique whisky glasses of old and beautiful design.

But the reason I'm writing about Lamparty was his electric iron. He made the hot chocolate on an electric iron turned upside down. Each ack-ack battery had a portable generator, so Lamparty just plugged in. His sister had sent him the iron two years back when he was in a camp near Chicago, and he had carried it ever since. Once upon a time he used to press his pants with it, but a guy with pressed pants in Normandy during the fighting would probably have been shot as a spy, so Lamparty was cooking with his iron.

7/22/44
Somewhere in France

I'm sending this column for some rainy day when the regular piece doesn't get through on time.

This one contains a few odds and ends which I didn't get down before about our invasion voyage across the Channel to France.

I came on a Navy LST which was a veteran of Sicily and Italy. She went up to England during the winter and had just been lying around since then.

She has a very fine crew, from the captain on down. Most of the crew have been through other amphibious campaigns, but there is a new batch of gunners who have been in the Navy only since December and who had never been shot at before our crossing.

The skipper is Lieut. John D. Walker Jr. of Houlton, Me. He is a gentle, courteous bachelor of 35, fine-looking, fine-minded, and beloved by his whole crew. Morale is high on this ship. A sailor will get you aside and tell you what a fine ship it has been since Walker took command.

Walker ran a Chevrolet and Cadillac agency in his hometown, but he is not the high-powered-salesman type at all. Aboard ship, his discipline is the kindly rather than the Simon Legree variety[28].

For example, there was a little exchange that I witnessed between him and the table waiter in the wardroom.

We had so many Army officers aboard that they practically crowed the Navy staff out of its own ship. At mealtime the few Navy colored boys were hard put to keep the tables waited on.

One of these was a little sailor nicknamed Peewee, who hasn't been out in the big world very much. At first you think he is sullen, but later you learn it is just a facial expression and he means all right. One day he went to Captain Walker and said,

'Captain, I guess you think I'm grouchy, but it ain't that, it's just that I'm worrying all the time.'

---

28. In the book Uncle Sam's Cabin, *Simon Legree was a brutal and immoral slave owner. By extension, his name became synonymous to harshness.*

Captain Walker had been trying to teach Peewee some nice dining-room manners. Trying to teach him to put things before his guests delicately, and not to jostle the guests or throw things at them.

One day, I was eating next to the captain, and an Army colonel was at the same table. Peewee wanted the colonel to get up and make room for somebody else, so he just reached over the colonel's shoulder and started mopping the table with a wet cloth, sort of pushing the colonel out of the way as he did so.

The colonel took the hint and got up and left. The captain saw it and was a little embarrassed. So, he said to Peewee, in a very kindly voice,

'Peewee, you kind of bruised the colonel, didn't you?'

And Peewee, not getting the subtle hint, and taking the captain literally, replied,

'No, sir, I didn't push him hard enough to hurt him.'

The captain just shook his head in despair and went on eating

Among the Army personnel aboard our ship was Capt. Warren Pershing, son of General Pershing[29]. The captain, who is not a professional soldier at all, started out as a private in this war. He is in the Engineers.

He is a tall, blond, regular fellow and everybody likes him. He leans over backward not to trade on his father's name. He doesn't speak of the General unless you ask him.

---

29. General John J. Pershing was Commander in Chief of the American troops sent to France during the First World War.

I asked if the General was still at Walter Reed Hospital[30]. He said yes, and that his father was very excited because they had just built him a penthouse on the hospital roof.

I have been told that despite his age and poor health General Pershing is very close to this war, and that some of our General Staff call on him almost daily for advice and counsel.

On the way across the Channel, Captain Pershing's commanding officer gave him a mission to perform the moment we hit the beach. His mission was to steal a bulldozer at a certain spot, right away.

I checked up a couple of days later to see if he had succeeded. He not only showed up with the bulldozer but with a hundred men as well. He even got the bulldozer without stealing it. Just talked somebody out of it.

7/24/44
Somewhere in Normandy

The cook on LST No, 92, on which I came to France, was a beefy, good-natured fellow named Edward Strucker, of (334 17th St.) Barberton, O. which is near Akron.

Cooking on these transport ships is a terrible job, for you suddenly have to turn out twice as much food as normally. But Eddie is not the worrying type, and he takes it all in his stride.

Eddie has a brother named Charles in the Army Engineers, and in the past year has been lucky enough to run into him four times - once in Africa, once in Sicily, and twice in Italy.

---

30. He suffered from senility and spent his last years at the Walter Reed Hospital in Washington, where he passed away in 1948, at the age of 88 years.

One of those small-world experiences happened to me, too, while on that ship. We lay at anchor in a certain harbor a couple of days before sailing for France. On the second day I was in the washroom shaving when a sailor came in and said there was a Commander Greene who wanted to see me in the captain's cabin.

The only Greene I could think of who might be a commander in the Navy was Lieut. Terry Greene, whom I had known in my Greenwich Village[31] days. You didn't know I ever had any Greenwich Village days? Well, don't get excited, because they weren't very lurid anyhow.

At any rate, I went to the captain's cabin, and sure enough it was the same Terry Greene all right. By some strange coincidence, we had both got 17 years older in the meantime.

Greene held a very important position in the convoy. He was tickled to death with his assignment, for he had been in the States almost the whole war and was about to go nuts for some action.

I haven't seen him on this side of the Channel to discuss it, but I'm afraid our trip over wasn't as exciting as he would have liked. But you can't please everybody, and it was just tame enough to suit me fine.

In your travels around the world if you ever happen to be sailing on LST No. 392 you might climb a ladder to a high platform astern which holds a big gun and look at the breech of the gun.

---

31. Greenwich Village is a district of New York, popular among artists and famous for its off-beat lifestyle.

There, written on each side of the barrel, you'll find my name. The boys in the gun crew asked if I would come up and write my name as big as I could on the gun, and then they would trace it over in red paint. Which they did. I'll be very much embarrassed now if the gun blows up on them. To say nothing of how they'll feel.

One of the gun crew is Seaman John Lepperd, of Hershey, Pa. He is about the oldest man in the crew. He is 34, and has three daughters - 17, 15 and 13 - and yet he got drafted last November and here he is sailing across the English Channel and helping shoot down German planes. It still seems a little odd to him. It is quite a contrast to the building game, which he had been in.

Also on this ship I ran into one of my home-towners from Albuquerque, Electrician's Mate Harold Lampton. His home actually is in Farmington, N.M. but he worked for the telephone company at Albuquerque, installing new phones. Now he is the electrician for this ship. He has been in the Navy for two years and overseas for more than a year. He is a tall, dark, quiet fellow who knows a great deal more about the Southwest than I do. He said he has driven past our house many times, and we had long nostalgic talks about the desert and Indian jewelry and sunsets. We are both tired of being where we are and we wish we were back on the Rio Grande.

Every LST in our convoy carried two or three barrage balloons. With each balloon was a soldier.

Among the soldiers I talked to on the LST were Corp. Loyce Gilbert, of Spring Hill, La., Pfc. Oscar Davis, of Troy, N.C., and Pvt Floyd Woodville, of (934 W. Lexington St.) Baltimore. They didn't seem especially apprehensive about going to war. I talked to them quite a while but never got much out of them except yes and no. Which was all right with me. I feel that way myself sometimes. Especially right now.

7/25/44
In Normandy

One of the things the layman doesn't hear much about is the Ordnance Department. In fact, it is one of the branches that even the average soldier is little aware of except in a vague way.

And yet the war couldn't keep going without it. For ordnance repairs all the vehicles of an army and furnishes all the ammunition for its guns.

Today there are more vehicles in the American sector of our beachhead than in the average-sized American city. And our big guns on an average heavy day are shooting up more than ten million dollars worth of ammunition. So, you see ordnance has a man-sized job.

Ordnance personnel is usually about six or seven percent of the total men of an army. That means we have many thousands of ordnancemen in Normandy. Their insignia is a flame coming out of a retort – nicknamed in the Army 'the flaming onion.'

Ordnance operates the ammunition dumps we have scattered about the beachhead. But much bigger than its ammunition mission is ordnance's job of repair. Ordnance has two hundred seventy-five thousand items in its catalog of parts, and the mere catalog itself covers a twenty-foot shelf.

In a central headquarters here on the beachhead a modern filing system housed in big tents keeps records on the number and condition of five hundred major items in actual use on the beachhead, from tanks to pistols.

We have scores and scores of separate ordnance companies at work on the beachhead – each of them a complete firm within itself, able to repair anything the Army uses.

Ordnance can lift a thirty-ton tank as easily as it can a bicycle. It can repair a blown-up jeep or the intricate breech of a mammoth gun. Some of its highly specialized repair companies are made up largely of men who were craftsmen in the same line in civil life. In these companies, you will find the average age is much above the army average. You will find craftsmen in their late forties, you'll find men with their own established businesses who were making thirty to forty thousand dollars a year back home and who are now wearing sergeant's stripes. You'll find great soberness and sincerity, plus the normal satisfaction that comes from making things whole again instead of destroying them.

You will find an IQ far above the average for the Army. It has to be that way or the work would not get done. You'll find mechanical work being done under a tree that would be housed in a $50,000 shop back in America. You'll find men working 16 hours a day, then sleeping on the ground, who because of their age don't even have to be here at all.

Ordnance is one of the undramatic branches of the Amy. They are the mechanics and the craftsmen, the fixers and the suppliers. But their job is vital. Ordinarily they are not in a great deal of danger. There are times on newly won and congested beachheads when their casualty rate is high, but once the war settles down and there is room for movement and dispersal, it is not necessary or desirable for them to do their basic work within gun range.

Our ordnance branch in Normandy has had casualties. It has two small branches which will continue to have casualties - its bomb-disposal squads and its retriever companies that go up to pull out crippled tanks under fire.

But outside of those two sections, if your son or husband is in ordnance in France, you can feel fairly easy about his returning to you. I don't say that to belittle ordnance in any way but to ease your worries if you have someone in this branch of the service oversea.

Ordnance is set up in a vast structure of organization the same as any other army command. The farther back you go, the bigger become the outfits and the more elaborately equipped and more capable of doing heavy, long-term work.

Every infantry or armored division has an ordnance company with it all the time. This company does quick repair jobs. What it hasn't time or facilities for doing it hands on back to the next echelon in the rear.

The division ordnance companies hit the beach on D-Day. The next echelon back began coming on D-Day plus four. The great heavy outfits arrived somewhat later.

Today the wreckage of seven weeks of war is all in hand, and in one great depot after another it is being worked out - repaired or rebuilt or sent back for salvage until everything possible is made available again to our men who do the fighting. In later columns I'll take you along to some of these repair companies that do the vital work.

7/26/44
Somewhere in Normandy

Let's go to what the ordnance branch calls one of its 'mobile maintenance companies.'

This type company repairs jeeps, light trucks, small arms and light artillery. It does not take tanks, heavy trucks or big guns. The company is bivouacked around the hedgerows of a large, grassy L-shaped pasture. There are no trees in the pasture. There is nothing in the center except grazing horses. No man or vehicle walks or drives across the pasture. Always they stick to the tree-high hedgerows.

It is hard to conceive that here in the thin, invisible line around the edges of this empty pasture there is a great machine shop with nearly 200 men working with wrenches and welding torches, that six teams of auto mechanics are busy, that the buzz of urgent labor goes on through all the daylight hours.

Actually, there is little need for such perfect camouflage for this company is perhaps 10 miles behind the lines, and German planes never appear in the daytime. But it's a good policy to keep in practice on camouflage.

This is a proud company. It was the first one to land in France - first, that is, behind the companies actually attached to divisions. It landed on D-Day plus 2 and lost three men killed and seven wounded when a shell hit their ship as they were unloading.

For five days it was the only ordnance company of its type ashore. Its small complement, whose job in theory is to back up only one division in medium repair work, carried all repair work for four divisions until help arrived.

The company had a proud record in the last war, being in nine major engagements. And it has a sentimental little coincidence in its history, too. In 1917 and in 1943, it left America for France on the same date, Dec. 12.

In one corner of the pasture is the command post tent where two sergeants and two officers work at folding tables and keep the records so necessary in ordnance.

A first lieutenant is in command of the company, assisted by five other lieutenants. Their standby is Warrant Officer Ernest Pike of Savoy, Tex., who has been in the Army 15 years, 13 of them with this very company.

What he doesn't know about practical ordnance you could put in a dead German's eye.

In another corner of the pasture is a mess truck with its field kitchens under some trees. Here the men of the company line up for meal with mess kits, officers as well as men, and eat sitting on the grass.

The officers lounge on the grass in a little group apart and when they finish eating they light cigarets and play a while with some cute little French puppies they found in German strong points, or traded soap and cigarets for. The officers know the men intimately and if they are in a hurry and have left their messkits behind, they just borrow one from some soldier who has finished eating.

A company of this kind is highly mobile. It can pack up and be underway in probably less than an hour.

Yet ordnance figures as a basic policy that its companies must not move oftener than every six days if they are to work successfully. They figure one day for moving, one for settling down and four days of full-time work, then move forward again.

If, at any time, the fighting army ahead of them gets rolling faster than this rate, the ordnance companies begin leap-frogging each other, one working while another of the same type moves around it and sets up.

Their equipment is moved in trucks and trailers. Some trucks are machine shops, others are supply stores. Some plain trucks are for hauling miscellaneous stuff.

Once set up, the men sleep on the ground in pup tents along the hedge with foxholes dug deep and handy. But usually, their greatest enemy is the hordes of mosquitoes that infest the hedgerows at night.

The more skilled men work at their benches and instruments inside the shop trucks. The bulk of the work outside is done under dark green canvas canopies stretched outward from the hedgerows and held taut on upright poles, their walls formed of camouflage nets.

Nothing but a vague blur is visible from a couple of hundred yards away. You have to make a long tour clear around the big pasture, nosing in under the hedge and camouflage nets to realize anything is going on at all.

In the far distance, you can hear a faint rumble of big guns, and overhead all day our own planes roar comfortingly.

But outside those fringes of war, it is as peaceful in this Normandy field as it would be in a pasture in Ohio. Why even the three liberated horses graze contentedly on the ankle-high grass, quite indifferent to the fact that this peaceful field is a part of the great war machine that will destroy their recent masters.

7/27/44
Somewhere in Normandy

Then I moved over to an ordnance evacuation company.

These men handle the gigantic trucks, the long, low trailers and the heavy wreckers that go out to haul back crippled tanks and wrecked anti-tank guns from the battlefield.

The Ordnance Branch's policy on these wrecking companies is that if they don't have a casualty now and then, or collect a few shrapnel marks on their vehicles, then they're not doing their job efficiently.

Tanks must be retrieved just as quickly as possible after they have been shot up. In the first place, we don't want the Germans to get them; secondly, we want to get them repaired and back in action for ourselves right away.

The job of an ordnance evacuation company is often frightening although this company's casualties have been amazingly low. In fact, they've had only four and it's still a mystery what happened to them.

The four left one day in a jeep, just on a normal trip. They didn't come back. No trace could be found. Three weeks later two of them came in - just discharged from a hospital. On the same day a letter came from the third – from a hospital in England. Nothing yet has been heard from the fourth.

And the strange part is that neither the two who returned nor the one who wrote from England can remember a thing about it. They were just riding along in their jeep and the next thing they woke up in a hospital. All three were wounded, but how they don't know. Friends suppose it was a shell hit.

At any rate, a sergeant in charge of one section of the mammoth movers, known as M-19s, took me around to see some of his crewmen. They all go by the name of 'The Diesel Boys.'

Their vehicle is simply a gigantic truck with a long, skeletonized trailer behind.

Like all our army over here, they were strung out around the hedgerows of the field under camouflage nets, with the middle grassy fields completely empty.

My friend was Sergt. Milton Radcliff of (111 N. 13th St.) Newark, O. He used to be a furnace operator for the Owen Corning Fiberglas Co. there. He and all the other former employees still get a letter every two weeks from the company, assuring them their jobs will still be there when they return. And Radcliff, for one, is going to take his when he gets back.

Sergt. Vann Jones of (1712 Princeton ave.) Birmingham, Ala. crawled out of his tent and sat Indian fashion on the ground with us. On the other side of our pasture lay the silver remains of a transport plane that had come to a mangled despair on the morning of D-Day.

It was a peaceful and sunny evening, quite in contrast to most of our days, and we sat on the grass and watched the sun go down in the east, which we all agreed was a hell of a place for the sun to be going down. Either we were turned around or France is a funny country.

The other boys told me later that Sergeant Jones used to be the company cook, but he wanted to see more action so he transferred to the big wreckers and is now in command of one.

His driver is a smiling, tall young fellow, with clipped hair, named Dallas Hudgens from Stonewall, Ga. He was feeling stuffed as a pig, for he'd just got a big ham sent him from home and had been having at it with a vengeance.

There are long lulls when the retriever boys don't have anything to do besides work on their vehicles. They hate these periods and get restless. Some of them spend their time fixing up their tents homelike, even though they may have to move the next day.

One driver even had a feather bed he had picked up from a French family. The average soldier can't carry a feather bed around with him, but the driver of an M-19 could carry ten thousand feather beds and never know the difference.

The boys are all pretty proud of their company. They said they did such good work in the early days of the invasion that they were about to be put up for Presidential Citation[32]. But one day they got in a bomb crater and started shooting captured German guns at the opposite bank just for fun, which is against the rules, so the proposal was torn up. They just laugh about it - which is about all a fellow can do.

Corp. Grover Anderson of Anniston, Ala., is one of the drivers. He swears by his colossal machine but cusses it, too. You see the French roads are narrow for heavy two-way military traffic and an M-19 is big and awkward and slow.

---

32. The Presidential Unit Citation is a decoration awarded to an American (or Allied) unit for acts of 'gallantry, determination and esprit de corps in accomplishing its mission under extremely difficult and hazardous conditions'.

'You get so damn mad at it,' Anderson says, 'because convoys pile up behind you and can't get around and you know everybody's hating you and that makes you madder. They're aggravating, but if you let me leave the trailer off I can pull anything out of anywhere with it.'

Anderson has grown a red goatee which he is not going to shave off till the war is won. He used to be a taxi driver; that's another reason he finds an M-19 so 'aggravating.'

'Because it hasn't got a meter on it?' I asked.

'Or maybe because you don't have any female passengers,' another driver said.

To which Brother Anderson had a wholly satisfactory GI reply.

He said '---' (remainder of column voluntarily censored) -.

7/27/44
Somewhere in Normandy

At the edge of a pasture, sitting cross-legged on the grass or on low boxes as though they were at a picnic, are 13 men in greasy soldiers' coveralls.

Near them on one side is a shop truck with a canvas canopy stretched out from it, making a sort of patio alongside the truck. And under this canopy and all over the ground are rifles - rusty and muddy and broken rifles.

This is the small arms section of our medium ordnance company. To this company comes daily in trucks they picked up, rusting rifles of men killed or wounded, and rifles broken in ordinary service. There are dozens of such companies.

This company turns back around a hundred rifles a day to its division, all shiny and oily and ready to shoot again.

They work on the simple salvage system of taking good parts off one gun and placing them on another. To do this, they work like a small assembly plant.

The first few hours of the morning are given to taking broken rifles apart. They don't try to keep the parts of each gun together. All parts are alike and transferable; hence they throw each type into a big steel pan full of similar parts. At the end of the job, they have a dozen or so pans, each filled with the same kind of part.

Then the whole gang shifts over and scrubs the parts. They scrub in gasoline, using sandpaper for guns in bad condition after lying out in the rain and mud.

When everything is clean, they take the good parts and start putting them back together and making guns out of them again.

When all the pans are empty, they have a stack of rifles – good rifles, all ready to be taken back to the front.

Of the parts left over some are thrown away quite beyond repair. But others are repairable and go into the section's shop truck for working on with lathes and welding torches, Thus the division gets 100 reclaimed rifles a day, in addition to the brand-new ones issued to it.

And believe me, during the first few days of our invasion, men at the front needed these rifles with desperation. Repairmen tell you how our paratroopers and infantrymen would straggle back, dirty and hazy-eyed with fatigue, and plead like a child for a new rifle immediately so they could get back to the front and 'get at them sonsabitches.'

One paratrooper brought in a German horse he had captured and offered to trade it for a new rifle, he needed it so badly. During those days, the men in our little repair shop worked all hours trying to fill the need.

I sat around on the grass and talked to these rifle repairmen most of one forenoon. They weren't working so frenziedly then for the urgency was not so dire, but they kept steadily at it as we talked.

The head of the section is Sergt. Edward Welch of Watts, Okla. who used to work in the oil fields. Just since the Invasion, he's invented a gadget that cleans rust out of a rifle barrel in a few seconds whereas it used to take a man about 20 minutes.

Sergeant Watts did it merely by rigging up a swivel shaft on the end of an electric drill and attaching a cylindrical wire brush to the end. So now you just stick the brush in the gun barrel and press the button on the drill. It whirls and in a few seconds all rust is ground out. The idea has been turned over to other ordnance companies.

The soldiers do a lot of kidding as they sit around taking rusted guns apart. Like soldiers everywhere they razz each other constantly about their home states. A couple were from Arkansas, and, of course, they took a lot of hillbilly razzing about not wearing shoes till they got in the Army and so on.

One of them was Corp. Herschel Grimsley of Springdale, Ark. He jokingly asked if I'd put his name in the paper. So, I took a chance and joked back, 'Sure,' I said, 'expect I didn't know anybody in Arkansas could read?'

Everybody laughed loudly at this scintillating wit, most of all Corporal Grimsley who can stand anything.

Later Grimsley was telling me how paratroopers used to come in and just beg for another rifle. And he expressed the sincere feeling of the men throughout ordnance, the balance weighing of their own fairly safe job, when he said, 'Them old boys at the front have sure got my sympathy. Least we can do is work our fingers off to give them the stuff.'

The original stack of muddy, rusted rifles is a touching pile. As gun after gun comes off the stack you look to see what is the matter with it.

Rifle butt split by fragments; barrel dented by bullet; trigger knocked off; whole barrel splattered with shrapnel marks; guns gray from the slime of weeks in swamp mud, faint dark splotches of blood still showing.

You wonder what became of each owner; you pretty well know.

Infantrymen, like soldiers everywhere, like to put names on their equipment. Just as a driver paints a name on his truck so does a doughboy carve his name or initials on his rifle butt.

You get crude whittlings of initials in the hard walnut stocks and unbelievably craftsmanlike carvings of soldiers' names, and many and many names of girls.

The boys said the most heart-breaking rifle they'd found was one of a soldier, who had carved a hole about silver dollar size and put his wife's or girl's picture in it, and sealed it over with a crystal of flexiglass.

They don't, of course, know who he was or what happened to him. They only know the rifle was repaired and somebody else is carrying it now, picture and all.

7/29/44
Somewhere in Normandy

It was just beginning dusk when the order came. A soldier came running up the pasture and said there was a call for our ordnance evacuation company to pull out some crippled tanks.

We had been sitting on the grass and we jumped up and ran down the slope. Waiting at the gate stood an M-19 truck and behind it a big wrecker with a crane.

The day had been warm, but dusk was bringing a chill, as always. One of the soldiers loaned me his mackinaw.

Soldiers stood stop their big machine with a stance of impatience, like firemen waiting to start. We pulled out through the hedgerow gate onto the main macadam highway. It was about 10 miles to the frontlines.

'We should make it before full darkness,' one of the officers said.

We went through shattered Carentan and on beyond for miles. Then we turned off at an angle in the road. 'This is Purple Heart Corner,' the officer said[33].

Beyond there the roadside soldiers thinned out. Traffic ceased altogether. With an increasing tempo, the big guns crashed around us. Hedges began to make weird shadows. You peered closely at sentries in every open hedge gate just out of nervous alertness.

The smell of death washed past us in waves as we drove on. There is nothing worse in war than the foul odor of death. There is no last vestige of dignity in it.

We turned up a gravel lane and drove slowly. The dusk was deepening. A gray stone farmhouse sat dimly off the road. A little yard and driveway semicircled in front of it. Against the front of the house stood five German soldiers, facing inward, their hands above their heads. An American doughboy stood in the driveway with a tommy-gun pointed at them. We drove on for about 50 yards and stopped. The drivers shut off their diesel motors.

One officer went into an orchard to try to find where the tanks were. In wartime nobody ever knows where anything is.

---

33. The only place in Normandy attributed this epithet is Purple Heart Lane, a portion of the RN13 trunk road that passes over the marshes and four rivers between Saint-Côme-du-Mont and Carentan. In June 1944, the American parachutists from the 101st Airborne Division, entrusted with the mission of capturing Carentan, struggled to evacuate this sector, steadfastly defended by the Germans. They consequently nicknamed the area Purple Heart Lane, after the eponymous medal awarded to American soldiers killed or wounded in combat.
Could this be the spot Ernie Pyle talks of in his article? This seems unlikely if we follow the chronology of combat progression in the area. The mystery remains…

The rest of us waited along the road beside an old stone barn. Three jeeps were parked beside it. The dusk was deeper now.

Out of the orchards around us roared and thundered our own artillery. An officer lit a cigaret. A sergeant with a rifle slung on his shoulder walked up and said, 'You better put that out, sir. There's snipers all around and they'll shot at a cigaret.'

The officer crushed the cigaret in his fingers, not waiting to drop it to the ground, and said, 'Thanks.'

'It's for your own good,' the sergeant said, apologetically.

The only traffic past us was an occasional jeep rigged up with a steel framework above to carry two stretcher cases. Every few minutes a jeep would pass with its patient burdens, slowly and silently and almost as though it was feeling its way.

Somehow as darkness comes down in a land of great danger you want things hushed. People begin to talk in low voices and feet on jeep throttles tread less heavily.

An early German plane droned overhead, passed, turned, dived and his white tracers came slanting down out of the sky. We crouched behind a stone wall. He was half a mile away, but the night is big and bullets can go anywhere and you are nervous.

An armored car pulled around us, pulled into a ditch ahead and shut off its motor. They said it was there in case the German night patrols tried to filter through.

On ahead there were single rifle shots and the give and take of machine gun rattles - one fast and one slow, one German and one American. You wondered after each blast if somebody who was whole a moment ago, some utter stranger, was now lying in sudden new anguish up there ahead in the illimitable darkness.

A shell whined that old familiar wail and hit in the orchard ahead with a crash. I moved quickly around behind the barn.

'You don't like that?' inquired a soldier out of the dusk.

I said, 'No, do you?'

And he replied as honestly, 'I sure as hell don't.'

A sergeant came up the road and said, 'You can stay here if you want to, but they shell this barn every hour on the hour. They're zeroed in on it.'

We looked at our watches. It was five minutes till midnight. Some of our soldiers stood boldly out in the middle of the road talking. But you could sense some of us, who were less composed, easing close to the stone wall, even close to the motherhood of the big silent trucks. Then an officer came out of the orchard. He had the directions. We all gathered around and listened. We had to pack up, cross two pastures, turn down another lane and go forward from there.

We were to drag back two German tanks for fear the Germans might retrieve them during the night. We backed ponderously up the road, our powerful exhaust blowing up dust as we moved.

As we passed the gray stone farmhouse we could see five silhouettes, very faintly through the now almost complete night - five Germans still facing the gray farmhouse.

We came to a lane and pulled forward into the orchard very slowly for you could barely see now.

Even in the lightning flashes of the big guns you could barely see.

(More tomorrow)

7/31/44
Somewhere in Normandy

We drove slowly across the two pastures in the big M-19 retriever truck with which our ordnance evacuation company was to pick up two crippled German tanks. The wrecker truck followed us. It was just after midnight.

We came to a lane at the far side of the pasture. Nobody was there to direct us. The officers had gone on ahead. We asked a sentry if he knew where the German tanks were. He had never heard of them. We shut off the motors and waited.

I think everybody was a little on edge. We certainly had American troops ahead of us, but he didn't know how far. When things are tense like that you get impatient of monkeying around. You want to get the job done and get the hell out of there.

We waited about 10 minutes, and finally a sergeant came back and said for us to drive on up the road about half a mile. He climbed on to direct us. Finally, we came to a barnyard, pulled in, turned around and then very slowly backed on up the road toward the enemy lines. I stood on the steel platform behind the driver so I could see.

It was very dark and you could only make out vague shapes. You could see dark walls of hedges and between them lighter strips of gravel road. Finally, a huge black shape took form at one side of the road. It was the first of the German tanks. Just before we got to it, we could make out two dark stripes on either side of the road on the ground. They were the size and shape of dead men, but they were only forms and I couldn't tell for sure.

Being tense and anxious to get finished, I hoped our truck would take the first tank. But no. We passed by, of course, and went backing on up the road.

When you're nervous you feel even 12 inches closer to the front is too much and the noise of your motor sounds like all the clanging of hell, directing the Germans to you.

I knew it was foolish to be nervous. I know there was plenty of protection ahead. And yet there are times when you don't feel good to start with, you're uncomposed and the framework of your character is off balance, and you are weak inside. That's the way I was that night. Fortunately, I'm not always that way.

Finally, the dark shape of the second tank loomed up. Our officers and some men were standing in the road beside it. We backed to within about five feet of it, and the driver shut off his motor and we climbed down.

A layman would think all you have to do is to hook a chain to the tank and pull it out of the ditch. But we were there half an hour. It seemed like all night to me.

First it had to be gone over for booby traps. I couldn't help but admire our mechanics. They know these foreign tanks as well as our own.

One of them climbed down the hatch into the driver's seat and there in the dark, completely by feel, investigated the intricate gadgets of the cockpit and found just what shape it was in and told us the trouble.

It seemed that on this tank two levers at the driver's seat had been left in gear and they were so bent there was not room to shift them out of gear.

One man was sent back up the road to get a hacksaw from the wrecker truck so they could saw off the handles. After five minutes he came back and said there wasn't any hacksaw. Then they sent him back after a crowbar and that finally did the trick.

During this time, we stood in a group around the tank, about a dozen of us, just talking. Shells still roamed the dark sky, but they weren't coming as near as before.

There would be lulls of many minutes when there was hardly a sound but our own voices. Most everybody talked in low tones, yet in any group there's always somebody who can't bear to speak in anything less than foghorn proportions.

And now and then when they'd have to hammer on the tank it sounded as though a boiler factory had collapsed. I tried to counter-act this by not talking at all.

An officer asked if anybody had inspected the breech of the tank's 88 gun. It seems the Germans sometimes leave a shell in the gun, rigged up so it goes off when the tank is moved. Another officer said the breech was empty. So we started.

Slowly, we ground back down the road in low gear with our great, black, massive load rolling behind us. One soldier rode in the tank to steer it.

We'd planned to pull it a long way back. Actually, we pulled it only about half a mile, then decided to put it in a field for the night.

When we pulled into a likely pasture the sentry at the hedgerow gate wanted to know what we were doing and we told him, 'Leaving a German tank for th night.'

And the sentry, in a horrified voice, said, 'Good God, don't leave it here. They might come after it.' But leave it there we did, and damn glad to get rid of it, I assure you.

We drove home in the blackout, watching the tall hedgerows against the lighter sky for guidance. For mile the roads were as empty and silent as the farthest corner of a desert. The crash of the guns grew welcomely dimmer and dimmer until finally everything was nearly silent and it seemed there could be only peace in Normandy.

At last, we came to our own hedgerow gate. As we drove in the sentry said, 'Coffee's waiting at the mess tent.' They feed 24 hours a day in these outfits that work like firemen.

But my sleeping bag lay unrolled and waiting on the ground in a nearby tent. It was 3 a.m. With an almost childish gratitude at being there at all I went right to bed.

8/1/44
Somewhere in Normandy

I know of nothing in civilian life at home by which you can even remotely compare the contribution to his country made by the infantry soldier with his life of bestiality, suffering and death.

But I've just been with an outfit whose war work is similar enough to yours that I believe you can see the difference between life overseas and in America.

A Sherman tank repair workshop in a Normandy forest. © *Photo National Archives USA/Manche Departmental Archives 13 Num 1294*

This is the heavy ordnance company which repairs shot-up tanks, wrecked artillery, and heavy trucks.

These men are not in much danger. They work at shop benches with tools. Compared with the infantry, their life is velvet and they know it and appreciate it. But, compared with them, your life is velvet. That's what I'd like for you to appreciate.

These men are mostly skilled craftsmen. Many of them are above military age. Back home they made big money. Their jobs here are fundamentally the same as those of you at home who work in war plants. It's only the environment that is different.

These men don't work seven, eight, or nine hours a day. They work from 7 in the morning until darkness comes at night. They work from 12 to 16 hours a day.

You have beds and bathrooms. These men sleep on the ground and dig a trench for their toilets.

You have meals at the table. These men eat from messkits, sitting on the grass. You have pyjamas and places to go on Sunday. These men sleep in their underwear, and they don't even know when Sunday comes. They have not sat in a chair for weeks. They live always outdoors, rain and shine.

In the War World, their life is not bad. By peacetime standards it is outrageous. But they don't complain - because they are close enough to the front to see and appreciate the desperate need of the men they are trying to help. They work with an eagerness and an intensity that is thrilling to see.

This company works under a half-acre grove of trees and along the hedgerows of a couple of adjoining pastures. Their shops are in the trucks or put in the open under camouflage nets.

Most of their work seems unspectacular to describe. It just consists of welding steel plates in the sides of tanks, of changing the front end of a truck blown up by a mine or repairing the barrel of a big gun hit by a bazooka, of rewinding the coils of a radio, of welding new teeth in a gear.

It's the sincere way they go at it, and their appreciation of its need that impressed me.

Corp. Richard Kelso is in this company. His home is at (1238 Roscoe St.) Chicago.

He is an Irish man from the Old Sod. He apprenticed in Belfast as a machinist nearly 30 years ago. He went to America when he was 25 and now he is 45.

He still has folks in Ireland, but he didn't have a chance to get over there when he was stationed in England. He is thin and a little stooped, and the others call him Pop. He is quiet and intent and very courteous. He never did get married.

Kelso operates the milling machine in a shop truck. His truck is covered deep with extra strips of steel, for these boys pick up and hoard steel as some people might hoard money.

When I stopped to chat, Kelso had his machine grinding away on the rough tooth of the gearwheel of a tank.

The part that did the cutting was one he had improvised himself. In this business of war so much is unforeseen, so much is missing at the right moment that were it not for improvisation, wars would be lost.

Take these gearwheels for instance. Suppose a tank strips three teeth off some gear. The entire tank is helpless and out of action. They have no replacement wheels in stock. They have to repair the broken one.

So, they take it to their outdoor foundry, make a form, heat up some steel till it is molten, pour it in the form and mould a rough gear tooth which is then welded onto the stub of the broken-off tooth.

Now, this rough tooth has to be ground down to the fine dimensions of the other teeth and that is an exact job. At first, they didn't have the tools to do with.

But that didn't stop them. They hacked those teeth down with cold chisels and hand files. They put back into action 20 tanks by this primitive method, Then Kelso and Warrant Officer Henry Moser, of Johnstown, Pa created a part for their milling machine that would do the job faster and better.

That one little improvisation may have saved 50 Americans' lives, may have cost the Germans a hundred men, may even have turned the tide of a battle.

And it's being done by a man 45 years old wearing Corporal stripes who doesn't have to be over here at all and who could be making big money back home.

He too sleeps on the ground and works 16 hours a day, and is happy to do it - for boys who are dying are not 3,000 miles away and abstract; they are 10 miles away and very, very real.

He sees them when they come back, pleading like children for another tank, another gun. He knows how terribly they need the things that are within his power to give.

Somewhere in Normandy

An ordnance tank repair company gets some freakish jobs, indeed.

The other day, the company I was with had a tank destroyer roll in. There was nothing wrong, whatever wrong with it except the end of the gun barrel was corked tight with 2 ½ feet of wood.

What happened was they had been running along a hedgerow and as the turret operator swung his gun in a forward arc, they ran the end of the barrel smack into a big tree.

You would think the vehicle had to be going 100 miles an hour to plug the end of the barrel for 2 ½ feet simply by running into a tree. But it doesn't. This one was going only 20 miles an hour.

It took the ordnance boys four hours to dig the wood out with chisels and reamers. The inside of the barrel wasn't hurt a bit and it went right back into action.

A 3-inch anti-tank gun was brought in with a hole in the barrel about six inches back from the muzzle. The hole came from the inside. What happened was this: a German bazooka gunner fired a rocket at the anti-tank gun. It made one of those freakish hole-in-one hits - went right smack into the muzzle of the big gun.

About six inches inside, it went off and burned its way clear through the barrel. Nobody got hurt, but the barrel was unrepairable and was sent back to England for salvage.

A tank was brought in that had been hit twice on the same side within a few seconds. The entrance holes were about two feet apart. But on the opposite side of the tank where the shells came out, there was only one hole. The angle of fire had been such that the second shell went right through the hole made by the first one.

In another case, an 88 shell struck the thick steel apron that shields the breech of one of a tank's guns. The shell didn't go through. It hit at an angle and just scooped out a big chunk of steel about a foot long and six inches wide.

It's very improbable that in the whole war this same shield would get hit again in the same place. Yet they can't afford to take that chance, so the weakened armor had to be made strong again.

They took acetylene torches and cut out a plug around the weakened part with slanting sides the same as you'd plug a watermelon.

Then they fashioned a steel plate the same size and shape as the hole, and welded it in.

The result is that the plug fits into the hole like a wedge and it would be impossible for a shell to drive it in. It's really stronger now than it used to be.

One of the most surprising things I ran onto touring around scores of outdoor ordnance shops in Normandy was a mobile tire repair unit.

There already are half a dozen of these units here and more coming in. They fix anything from a motorcycle to truck tires. They don't bother with ordinary holes such as nail holes. Practically all their work is on tires damaged by shrapnel or bullets.

Each repair outfit consists of one officer and 15 men. They've been especially trained and their leaders usually were tiremen back in civil life.

They move in three trucks. When they set up, the three are backed to each other to form a T, thus making a shop with three wings. You get up to it on a portable staircase.

Outside on the ground, tires are stacked all around. One set of soldiers works all day with knives carving out the rubber around the damaged places. Then they take the tire inside, and a machine roughens the edges of the holes so the filling will stick.

Then they mould in fresh rubber and put the tire in one of three baking machines. It's hotter than blazes in there. It takes an hour and 45 minutes to bake each patch so you see they can't turn them out very fast.

They'll repair a tire that has up to six holes, but if it has more than that they send it back to England. A six-hole tire takes 10 ½ hours of baking. One unit can run off a maximum of about 65 tires daily. The unit I saw was set up in a former orchard and was so thoroughly camouflaged with nets you could hardly see it. The officer in charge was Lieut. George Schuchardt who has 'The Hawkinson Tread Service' in Nashville, Tenn.[34] His partner is running it while he's away.

His first sergeant is Stephen Hudak of (51 Flore ave.) Akron, of all places. He used to work for Firestone[35]. I've been finding more damned square pegs in square holes in this army lately. Something must be wrong.

8/3/44
Somewhere in Normandy

Mosquitoes are pretty bad in the swampy parts of Normandy. Especially along the hedgerows at night, they are ferocious.

Here in Normandy, they have something I've never seen before even in Alaska, the mosquito capital of the world.

When you drive along a Normandy road just before dusk, you'll see dark columns extending 200 and 300 feet straight up into the air above a treetop. These are columns of mosquitoes swarming like bees, each column composed of millions of them.

At first, I thought they were gnats, but old mosquito people assure me they are genuine, all-wool mosquitoes. In a half-

---

34. *Hawkinson is a chain of tyre skiving workshops, established in the United States since the 1930s.*
35. *The very first factory opened by the giant tyre firm Firestone was created in Akron.*

mile drive just before dusk, you'll see 20 of these columns. This is no cock and bull story; it's the truth.

Our troops are not equipped with mosquito nets, so they just have to scratch and scratch. The mosquitoes, fortunately, don't give you malaria, they merely drive you crazy.

One day at an ordnance company, I was talking with a soldier scrubbing rusted rifle barrels in a washtub of gasoline. His sleeves were rolled up and his arms were covered with great red bumps, They were mosquito bites.

As we talked this man said, 'Look at them mosquitoes hit that gasoline.'

And sure enough the mosquitoes were diving just like dive bombers but once they hit the gasoline they'd just fold up and died beautifully and floated on the surface.

***

In one small-arms repair section that I visited, the only man who knew or cared anything about guns before the war was a professional gun collector.

He was Sergt. Joseph. Toth of Mansfield, O. He was stripped down to his undershirt as the day was warm for a change. He was washing the walnut stocks of damaged rifles in a tub of water with a sponge.

Toth used to work at the Westinghouse Electric plant in Mansfield and he spent all his extra money collecting guns. He belongs to the Ohio Gun Collectors Assn.

He says each one of the gun collectors back in Ohio has a different specialty. Some collect pistols; some muzzleloaders.

His own hobby was machine pistols. He has 35 in his collection, some of them very expensive.

Ironically enough, he has not collected any guns over here at all, even though he's in a world of machine pistols and many pass through his hands.

'It isn't so much the collecting,' he says. 'I just like to take them down. When I monkey with a gun, I like to take it clear down and put it back together again.'

Toth also likes to talk. He'll talk all day. As the other boys say, if he could always have a new type machine pistol to take down and somebody to listen to him at the same time he'd constantly be the happiest man on earth.

***

Eggs are not plentiful enough in Normandy to supply the whole army, but a good scrounger can dig up a few each day. We buy them from farmers wives for six and eight cents apiece. We're hoping some day to buy some from a farmer's daughter.

These Normandy eggs are fine eggs, and about every fourth one is as big as a duck egg. The five men in our tent are all egg conscious, so we make it a practice to shop for eggs as we go about the country.

We pass up regular breakfast in the army mess and have our breakfast in our own tent every morning. By some inexplicable evolution of cruel fate, I have become the chef for this four-man crew of breakfast Gargantuans.

Those four plutocrats lie in their cots and snore while I get out at the crack of dawn and slave over two Coleman stoves, cooking their *oeufs* in real Normandy butter - fried, scrambled, boiled or poached, as suits the whims of their respective majesties.

Except when I'm away with troops, I've been at this despicable occupation now for two months. And although my clients are smart enough to keep me always graciously flattered about my culinary genius, I'm getting damn sick of the job.

So, someday I'm going to carry out the most diabolical scheme. I'll prepare, with the greatest care, the most delicious breakfast ever known in France - I'll have shirred humming-bird eggs and crisp French fried potatoes and corn-fed bacon, done to a turn, and grape jelly and autumn-brown toast and gallons and gallons of thick, luscious coffee.

Then I'll wake them up and I'll serve it to all four of them on a red platter. I'll serve it with a bow to Mr. Whitehead, and a curtsy to Mr. Liebling, and a 'Good morning to you, sir,' to Mr. Brandt, and a long salute to Mr. Gorrell. And after I've served it, I'll walk out casually as though I'm going up the hedgerow a little ways. But instead, I'll go on away and I'll never come back again as long as I live, never, not even if they put an ad in the paper, and they will all wither away to nothing from lack of sustenance, and eventually they will starve plumb to death in this faraway and strangely beautiful land. Ha, ha.

8/4/44
Somewhere in Normandy

One afternoon a couple of soldiers came around our camp to tell me about the strange experience that had just happened to them. They were brothers, and the night before they had run onto each other for the first time in more than two years.

They are Corp. John and Pvt. Edward O'Donnell of East Milton, Mass. John is an artilleryman and has been overseas more than two years, all through Africa and Sicily. Edward has been overseas only a couple of months. John is 22 and Edward 19.

The first Edward knew his brother was in the vicinity was when he saw some soldiers, wearing the patch of John's division, getting ready to take a bath at an outdoor shower the Army had set up.

He asked them where the division was and then began a several-hour hunt for his brother. John was attending an Army movie set up in a barn when Edward finally tracked him down. They sent in word for John to come out. When he got about halfway out and saw who was waiting, he practically knocked everybody out of their chairs getting to the back.

Their commanding officers gave them the next day off and they just roamed around with their tongues wagging - talking mostly about home.

***

That same afternoon, another soldier came by to say hello because his name is the same as mine. He is Pvt. Stewart Pyle of Orange, N.J. He is the driver in a car company, and now and then he gets an assignment to drive some very high officers. At least that will give him something to talk about to his grandchildren.

Private Pyle is married and had been overseas nine months. Try as we might, we couldn't establish any relationship. That might have been due to the fact that my name isn't Pyle at all, but Count Sforzo Chef Du Pont D'Artagnan.

Our family sprang from a long line of Norman milkmaids. We took the name Pyle after the Jones murder cases in 1739 - January, I think it was. My great-grandfather built the Empire State Building. Why am I telling you all this?

Department of Wartime Distorted Values - The other day a soldier offered to trade a French farmer three horses for three eggs. The soldier had captured the horses from the Germans. The trade didn't come off - the farmer already had three horses.

And... at one of our evacuation hospitals the other day, a wounded soldier turned over 90,000 francs, equivalent to $1,800. He'd picked them up in a captured German headquarters. The Army is now in the process of looking up regulations to see whether the soldier can keep the money.

***

In the very early days of the invasion, I said in this column that Capt. Ralph L. Haga of Prospect, Va. claimed to be the first chaplain ashore on D-Day.

Well, I got into trouble over that, because he wasn't. If I'd had any sense, I would have known better myself. The first chaplains on the beachhead were these who jumped with the paratroopers and there were a batch of them - I believe 17, altogether. They were in Normandy hours before Chaplain Haga touched the beach.

As one bunch of paratroopers wrote me, 'Our chaplains had already rendered their first consolation service in France before Captain Haga got his feet wet.' So all credit where credit is due.

***

One afternoon several weeks ago I went into Cherbourg with an infantry company and one of the doughboys gave me two cans of French sardines they'd captured from the Germans.

Right in the midst of battle is a funny place to be giving a man sardines, but this is a funny war. At any rate, I was grateful and I put them in my musette bag when I got back to my tent that night.

I forgot all about them.

The reason I mention it now is that last night I got a hungry spell and was rummaging around in the bag for candy or something and ran onto these sardines. They tasted mighty good.

8/5/44
In Normandy

A few days after D-Day you may remember we spoke in this column of five early phases of the continental invasion that would have to take place.

Phase No. .5 was to be the breakout from our beachhead after we'd held it secure long enough to build up vast quantities of troops and supplies behind us. And once we'd broken out of the ring of Germans trying to hold us in and completed Phase 5, the real war in Western Europe would begin.

Well, we're in Phase 5 now. At least we are while I'm writing this. Things are moving swiftly. You realize that several days elapse between the writing and the publication of this column. By the time you read this we may be out in the open and pushing into France.

Surely history will give a name to the battle that sent us boiling out of Normandy - some name comparable with St. Mihiel, or Meuse Argonne[36] of the last war. But to us, here on the spot at the time, it was known simply as 'the breakthrough.'

We correspondents could sense that a big drive was coming. There are many little ways you can tell without actually being told if you are experienced in war.

And then one evening Lieut. Gen. Omar Bradley, commanding all American troops in France, came to our camp and briefed us on the coming operation[37]. It would start, he said, on the first day we had three hours good flying weather in the forenoon.

We were all glad to hear the news. There isn't a correspondent over here, or soldier, or officer I ever heard of who hasn't complete and utter faith in General Bradley. If he felt we were ready for the push, that was good enough for us.

The General told us the attack would cover a segment of the German line west of St-Lo, about 2 1/3 miles wide. In that narrow segment we would have three infantry divisions, side by side. Right behind them would be another infantry and two armored divisions.

Once a hole was broken, the armored divisions would slam through several miles beyond then turn right toward the sea

---

36. Battle during the First World War in which the U.S. Army was intensively engaged.
37. Here, Pyle is clearly referring to Operation Cobra, launched on 25th July in the Saint-Gilles/Hébécrevon/Marigny sector. The breakthrough mentioned by Pyle is, of course, that of Avranches, during which - after Operation Cobra - the Americans broke through the German lines in the Manche area, progressed down towards Avranches, then paved the way towards liberating France's 'Great West'.

behind the Germans in that sector in the hope of cutting them off and trapping them.

The remainder of our line on both sides of the attack would keep the pressure on to hold the Germans in front of them so they couldn't send reinforcements against our big attack.

The attack was to open with a gigantic two-hour air bombardment by 1,800 planes - the biggest, I'm sure, ever attempted by air in direct support of ground troops.

It would start with dive bombers, then great four-motored heavies would come, and then mediums, then dive bombers again, and then the ground troops would kick off, with air fighters continuing to work ahead of them.

It was a thrilling plan to listen to. General Bradley didn't tell us the big thing - that this was Phase 5. But other officers gave us the word. They said, 'This is no limited objective drive. This is it. This is the big breakthrough.'

In war everybody contributes something, no matter how small or how far removed he may be. But on the frontline, this breakthrough was accomplished by four fighting branches of the services and I don't see truly how one could be given credit, above another.

None of the four could have done the job without the other three. The way they worked together was beautiful and precision-like, showering credit upon the missives and General Bradley's planning. The four branches were the Air Corps, Tanks, Artillery and Infantry.

I went with the infantry because it is my love, and because I suspected the tanks, being spectacular, might smother the credit due to the infantry. I teamed up with the Fourth Infantry

Division since it was in the middle of the forward three and spearheading the attack.

The first night behind the frontlines I slept comfortably on a cot in a tent at the division command post and met for the first time the Fourth's commander - Maj. Gen. Raymond O. Barton, a fatherly, kindly thoughtful, good soldier.

The second night I spent on the dirty floor of a rickety French farmhouse far up in the lines, with the nauseating odor of dead cows keeping me awake half the night.

The third night I slept on the ground in an orchard even farther up, snugly dug in behind a hedgerow so the 88s couldn't get at me so easily. And on the next day the weather cleared, and the attack was on. It was July 25.

If you don't have July 25 pasted in your hat, I would advise you to do so immediately. At least paste it in your mind. For I have a hunch that July 25 of the year. 1944 will be one of the great historic pinnacles of this war.

It was the day we began a mighty surge out of our confined Normandy spaces, the day we stopped calling our area the beachhead, and knew we were fighting a war across the whole expanse of France.

From that day onward, all dread possibilities and fears for disaster to our invasion were behind us. No longer was there any possibility of our getting kicked off. No longer could it be possible for fate, or weather, or enemy to wound us fatally; from that day onward, the future could hold nothing for us but growing strength and eventual victory.

For five days and nights during that historic period, I stayed at the front with our troops. And now, though it's slightly delayed,

I want to tell you about it in detail from day to day, if you will be that patient.

8/7/44
In Normandy

The great attack, when we broke out of the Normandy beachhead, began in the bright light of midday, not at the zero hour of a bleak and mysterious dawn as attacks are supposed to start in books.

The attack had been delayed from day to day because of poor flying weather and, on the final day we hadn't known for sure till after breakfast whether it was on or off again.

When the word came that it was on, the various battalion staffs of our regiment were called in from their command posts for a final review of the battle plan.

Each one was given a mimeographed sketch of the frontline area, showing exactly where and when each type of bomber was to hammer the German lines ahead of them. Another mimeographed page was filled with specific orders for the grand attack to follow.

Officers stood or squatted in a circle in a little apple orchard behind a ramshackle stone farmhouse of a poor French family who had left before us. The stonewall in the front yard had been knocked down by shelling, and through the orchards there were shell craters and tree limbs knocked off and trunks sliced by bullets. Some enlisted men sleeping the night before in the attic of the house got the shock of their lives when the thin floor collapsed and they fell down into the cowshed below.

Chickens and tame rabbits still scampered around the farmyard Dead cows lay all around in the fields.

The regimental colonel stood in the center of the officers and went over the orders in detail. Battalion commanders took down notes in little books.

The colonel said, 'Ernie Pyle is with the regiment for this attack and will be with one of the battalions, so you'll be seeing him.' The officers looked at me and smiled and I felt embarrassed.

Then Maj. Gen. Raymond O. Barton, Fourth Division Commander, arrived. The colonel called, 'Attention!' and everybody stood rigid until the General gave them, 'Carry on.'

An enlisted man ran to the mess truck and got a folding canvas stool for the General to sit on. He sat listening intently while the colonel wound up his instructions.

Then the General stepped into the center of the circle. He stood at a slouch on one foot with the other leg far out like a brace. He looked all around him as he talked. He didn't talk long. He said something like this, 'This is one of the finest regiments in the American Army. It was the last regiment out of France in the last war. It was the first regiment into France in this war[38]. It has spearheaded every one of the division's attacks in Normandy. It will spearhead this one. For many years this was my regiment and I feel very close to you, and very proud.'

The General's lined face was a study in emotion. Sincerity and deep sentiment were in every contour and they shone from

---

38. *The 8th Infantry Regiment, which comprised the very first waves of assault on Utah Beach on 6 June 1944.*

his eyes. General Barton is a man of deep affections. The tragedy of war, both personal and impersonal, hurts him. At the end his voice almost broke, and I for one had a lump in my throat. He ended, 'That's all. God bless you and good luck.'

Then we broke up and I went with one of the battalion commanders. Word was passed down by field phone, radio and liaison men to the very smallest unit of troops that the attack was on.

There was still an hour before the bombers, and three hours before the infantry were to move. There was nothing for the infantry to do but dig a little deeper and wait. A cessation of motion seemed to come over the countryside and all its brown-clad inhabitants - a sense of last-minute sitting in silence before the holocaust.

The first planes of the mass onslaught came over a little before 10 a.m. They were the fighters and dive bombers. The main road running crosswise in front of us was their bomb line. They were to bomb only on the far side of that road.

Our kickoff infantry had been pulled back a few hundred yards this side of the road. Everyone in the area had been given the strictest orders to be in foxholes, for high-level bombers can, and do quite excusably, make mistakes.

We were still in country so level and with hedgerows so tall there simply was no high spot - either hill or building - from where you could get a grandstand view of the bombing as we used to in Sicily and Italy. So, one place was as good as another unless you went right up and sat on the bomb line.

Having been caught too close to three things before, I compromised and picked a farmyard about 800 yards back of the kickoff line.

And before the next two hours had passed, I would have given every penny, every desire, every hope I've ever had to have been just another 800 yards further back.

8/8/44
In Normandy

Our frontlines were marked by long strips of colored cloth laid on the ground, and with colored smoke to guide our airmen during the mass bombing that preceded our breakout from the German ring that held us to the Normandy beachhead.

Dive bombers hit it just right. We stood in the barnyard of a French farm and watched them barrel nearly straight down out of the sky. They were bombing about half a mile ahead of where we stood.

They came in groups, diving from every direction, perfectly timed, one right after another. Everywhere you looked separate groups of planes were on the way down, or on the way back up, or slanting over for a dive, or circling, circling, circling over our heads, waiting for their turn.

The air was full of sharp and distinct sounds of cracking bombs and the heavy rips of the planes' machine guns and the splitting screams of diving wings. It was all fast and furious, but yet distinct as in a musical show in which you could distinguish throaty tunes and words.

And then a new sound gradually droned into our ears, a sound deep and all-encompassing with no notes in it - just a gigantic faraway surge of doom-like sound. It was the heavies. They came from directly behind us. At first, they were the merest dots in the sky. You could see clots of them against the far heavens, too tiny to count individually. They came on with a terrible slowness.

They came in flights of 12, three flights to a group and in groups stretched out across the sky. They came in 'families' of about 70 planes each.

Maybe these gigantic waves were two miles apart, maybe they were 10 miles, I don't know. But I do know they came in a constant procession and I thought it would never end. What the Germans must have thought is beyond comprehension.

Their march across the sky was slow and studied. I've never known a storm, or a machine, or any resolve of man that had about it the aura of such a ghastly relentlessness. You had the feeling that, even had God appeared beseechingly before them in the sky with palms outward to persuade them back, they would not have had within them the power to turn from their irresistible course.

I stood with a little group of men, ranging from colonels to privates, back of the stone farmhouse.

Slit trenches were all around the edges of the farmyard and a dugout with a tin roof was nearby. But we were so fascinated by the spectacle overhead that it never occurred to us that we might need the foxholes.

The first huge flight passed directly over our farmyard and others followed. We spread our feet and leaned far back trying to look straight up, until our steel helmets fell off. We'd cup our fingers around our eyes like field glasses for a clearer view.

And then the bombs came. They began ahead of us as the crackle of popcorn and almost instantly swelled into a monstrous fury of noise that seemed surely to destroy all the world ahead of us.

From then on for an hour and a half that had in it the agonies of centuries, the bombs came down. A wall of smoke and dust erected by them grew high in the sky. It filtered along the ground back through our own orchards. It sifted around us and into our noses. The bright day grew slowly dark from it.

By now everything was an indescribable cauldron of sounds. Individual noises did not exist. The thundering of the motors in the sky and the roar of bombs ahead filled all the space for noise on earth. Our own heavy artillery was crashing all around us, yet we could hardly hear it.

The Germans began to shoot heavy, high ack-ack. Great black puffs of it by the score speckled the sky until it was hard to distinguish smoke puffs from planes.

And then someone shouted that one of the planes was smoking. Yes, we could all see it. A long faint line of black smoke stretched straight for a mile behind one of them.

And as we watched there was a gigantic sweep of flame over the plane. From nose to tail it disappeared in flame, and it slanted slowly down and banked around the sky in great wide curves, this way and that way, as rhythmically and gracefully as in a slow-motion waltz.

Then suddenly it seemed to change its mind and it swept upward, steeper and steeper and ever slower until finally it seemed poised motionless on its own black pillar of smoke. And then just as slowly it turned over and dived for the earth

- a golden spearhead on the straight black shaft of its own creation - and it disappeared behind the treetops.

But before it was done there were more cries of, 'There's another one smoking and there's a third one now.'

Chutes came out of some of the planes. Out of some came no chutes at all. One of white silk caught on the tail of a plane. Men with binoculars could see him fighting to get loose until flames swept over him, and then a tiny black dot fell through space, all alone.

And all that time, the great flat ceiling of the sky was roofed by all the others that didn't go down, plowing their way forward as if there were no turmoil in the world.

Nothing deviated them by the slightest. They stalked on, slowly and with a dreadful pall of sound, as though they were seeing only something at a great distance and nothing existed in between. God, how you admired those men up there and sickened for the ones who fell.

8/9/44
In Normandy

It is possible to become so enthralled by some of the spectacles of war that you are momentarily captivated away from your own danger.

That's what happened to our little group of soldiers as we stood in a French farmyard, watching the mighty bombing of the German lines just before our breakthrough.

But that benign state didn't last long. As we watched, there crept into our consciousness a realization that windrows of exploding bombs were easing back toward us, flight by flight, instead of gradually forward, as the plan called for.

Then we were horrified by the suspicion that those machines, high in the sky and completely detached from us, were aiming their bombs at the smokeline on the ground - and a gentle breeze was drifting the smokeline back over us![39]

An indescribable kind of panic comes over you at such times. We stood tensed in muscle and frozen in intellect, watching each flight approach and pass over us, feeling trapped and completely helpless.

And then, all of an instant, the universe became filled with a gigantic rattling as of huge, dry seeds in a mammoth dry gourd. I doubt that any of us had ever heard that sound before, but instinct told us what it was. It was bombs by the hundred, hurtling down through the air above us.

Many times, I've heard bombs whistle or swish or rustle, but never before had I heard bombs rattle. I still don't know the explanation of it. But it is an awful sound.

We dived. Some got in a dugout. Others made foxholes and ditches and some got behind a garden wall - although which side would be 'behind' was anybody's guess.

---

39. Initially scheduled on 24th July, the Cobra bombardments were postponed at the last minute due to unfavourable weather conditions. Too late for several bomber planes that had already taken off and couldn't be called back to base. They dropped their bombs on their targets. Erroneous targets for the 30th U.S. Infantry Division bore the brunt of the attack, with 25 dead and 130 wounded. The following day, on 25th July, the operation was resumed despite little improvement in the weather. And once more, the American bombers hit the 30th Division, causing a further 111 deaths and 490 wounded. Such are the dramatic errors Pyle describes in this article.

I was too late for the dugout. The nearest place was a wagon-shed which formed one end of the stone house. The rattle was right down upon us. I remember hitting the ground flat, all spread out like the cartoons of people flattened by steam rollers, and then squirming like an eel to get under one of the heavy wagons in the shed.

An officer whom I didn't know was wriggling beside me. We stopped at the same time, simultaneously feeling it was hopeless to move farther. The bombs were already crashing around us.

We lay with our heads slightly up - like two snakes - staring at each other. I know it was in both our minds and in our eyes, asking each other what to do. Neither of us knew. We said nothing.

We just lay sprawled, gaping at each other in a futile appeal, our faces about a foot apart, until it was over.

There is no description of the sound and fury of those bombs except to say it was chaos, and a waiting for darkness. The feeling of the blast was sensational. The air struck you in hundreds of continuing flutters. Your ears drummed and rang. You could feel quick little waves of concussions on your chest and in your eyes.

At last, the sound died down and we looked at each other in disbelief. Gradually we left the foxholes and sprawling places and came out to see what the sky had in store for us. As far as we could see, other waves were approaching from behind.

When a wave would pass a little to the side of us, we were garrulously grateful, for most of them flew directly overhead. Time and again, the rattle came down over us. Bombs struck in the orchard to our left. They struck in orchards ahead of us. They struck as far as half a mile behind us. Everything about us was shaken but our group came through unhurt.

I can't record what any of us actually felt or thought during those horrible climaxes. I believe a person's feelings at such times are kaleidoscopic and uncatalogable. You just wait, that's all. You do remember an inhuman tenseness of muscle and nerves.

An hour or so later I began to get sore all over, and by mid-afternoon my back and shoulders ached as though I'd been beaten with a club. It was simply the result of muscles tensing themselves too tight for too long against anticipated shock. And I remember worrying about War Correspondent Ken Crawford, a friend from back in the old Washington days, who I knew was several hundred yards ahead of me.

As far as I know, he and I were the only two correspondents with the Fourth Division. I didn't know who might be with the divisions on either side - which also were being hit as we could see.

Three days later, back at camp, I learned that AP Photographer Bede Irvin had been killed in the bombing and that Ken was safe.

We came out of our ignominious sprawling and stood up again to watch. We could sense that by now the error had been caught and checked. The bombs again were falling where they were intended, a mile or so ahead.

Even at a mile away, a thousand bombs hitting within a few seconds can shake the earth and shatter the air where you are standing. There was still a dread in our hearts, but it gradually eased as the tumult and destruction moved slowly forward.

8/10/44
In Normandy

With our own personal danger past, our historic air bombardment of the German lines holding us in the Normandy beachhead again became a captivating spectacle to watch.

By now it was definite that the great waves of four-motored planes were dropping their deadly loads exactly in the right place.

And by now two Mustang fighters, flying like a pair of doves, patrolled back and forth, back and forth, just in front of each oncoming wave of bombers, as if to shout to them by their mere presence that here was not the place to drop - wait a few seconds, wait, a few more seconds.

And then we could see a flare come out of the belly of one plane in each flight, just after they had passed over our heads.

The flare shot forward, leaving smoke behind it in a vivid line, and then began a graceful, downward curve that was one of the most beautiful things I've ever seen.

It was like an invisible crayon drawing a rapid line across the canvas of the sky, saying in a gesture for all to see, 'Here! Here is where to drop. Follow me.'

And each succeeding flight of oncoming bombers obeyed, and in turn dropped its own hurtling marker across the illimitable heaven to guide those behind.

Long before now, the German ack-ack guns had gone out of existence. We had counted three of our big planes down in spectacular flames, and I believe that was all. The German ack-ack gunners either took to their holes or were annihilated.

How many waves of heavy bombers we put over I have no idea. I had counted well beyond 400 planes when my personal distraction obliterated any capacity or desire to count.

I only know that 400 was just the beginning. There were supposed to be 1,800 planes that day, and I believe it was announced later that there were more than 3,000.

It seemed incredible to me that any German could come out of that bombardment with his sanity. When it was over, even I was grateful in a chastened way I had never experienced before, for just being alive.

I thought an attack by our troops was impossible now, for it is an unnerving thing to be bombed by your own planes.

During the bad part, a colonel I had known a long time was walking up and down behind the farmhouse snapping his fingers and saying over and over to himself, 'Goddamit, goddammit!

As he passed me once, he stopped and stared and said, 'Goddamit!" And I said, "There can't be any attack now, can there?' And he said, 'No,' and began walking again, snapping his fingers and tossing his arm as though he was throwing rocks at the ground.

The leading company of our battalion was to spearhead the attack 40 minutes after our heavy bombing ceased. The company had been hit directly by our bombs. Their casualties including casualties in shock, were heavy. Men went to pieces and had to be sent back. The company was shattered and shaken.

And yet Company B attacked - and on time, to the minute. They attacked, and within an hour they sent word back that they had advanced 800 yards through German territory and were still going. Around our farmyard, men with stars on their shoulders almost wept when the word came over the portable radio. The American soldier can be majestic when he needs to be.

There is one more thing I want to say before we follow the ground troops on deeper into France in the great push you've been reading about now for days.

I'm sure that back in England that night other men - bomber crews - almost wept, and maybe they did really, in the awful knowledge that they had killed our own American troops. But I want to say this to them. The chaos and the bitterness there in the orchards and between the hedgerows that afternoon have passed. After the bitterness came the sober remembrance that the Air Corps is the strong right arm in front of us. Not only at the beginning, but ceaselessly and everlastingly, every moment of the faintest daylight, the Air Corps is up there banging away ahead of us.

Anybody makes mistakes. The enemy makes them just the same as we do. The smoke and confusion of battle bewilder us all on the ground as well as in the air. And in this case the percentage of error was really very small compared with the colossal storm of bombs that fell upon the enemy.

The Air Corps has been wonderful throughout this invasion, and the men on the ground appreciate it.

8/11/44
On the Western Front

I know that all of us correspondents have tried time and again to describe to you what this weird hedgerow fighting in northwestern France has been like.

But I'm going to go over it once more, for we've been in it two months and some of us feel that this is the two months that broke the German Army in the west.

This type of fighting is always in small groups, so let's take as an example one company of men. Let's say they are working forward on both sides of a country lane, and this company is responsible for clearing the two fields on either side of the road as it advances. That means you have only about one platoon to a field. And with the company's understrength from casualties, you might have no more than 25 or 30 men in a field.

Over here, the fields are usually not more than 50 yards across and a couple of hundred yards long. They may have grain in them, or apple trees, but mostly they are just pastures of green grass, full of beautiful cows. The fields are surrounded on all sides by immense hedgerows which consist of an ancient earthen bank, waist-high, all matted with roots, and out of which grow weeds, bushes, and trees up to 20 feet high.

The Germans have used these barriers well. They put snipers in the trees. They dig deep trenches behind the hedgerows and cover them with timber, so that it is almost impossible for artillery to get at them.

Sometimes, they will prop up machine guns with strings attached, so they can fire over the hedge without getting out of their holes. They even cut out a section of the hedgerow and hide a big gun or a tank in it, covering it with brush.

Also, they tunnel under the hedgerows from the back and make the opening on the forward side just large enough to stick a machine gun through.

But mostly, the hedgerow pattern is this: a heavy machine gun hidden at each end of the field and infantrymen, hidden all along the hedgerow with rifles and machine pistols.

Now it's up to us to dig them out of there. It's a slow and cautious business, and there is nothing very dashing about it. Our men don't go across the open fields in dramatic charges such as you see in the movies. They did at first, but they learned better.

They go in tiny groups, a squad or less, moving yards apart and sticking close to the hedgerows on either end of the field. They creep a few yards, squat, wait, then creep again.

If you could be right up there between the Germans and the Americans you wouldn't see very many men at any one time - just a few here and there, always trying to keep hidden. But you would hear an awful lot of noise.

Our men were taught in training not to fire until they saw something to fire at. But that hasn't worked in this country, because you see so little. So, the alternative is to keep shooting constantly at the hedgerows. That pins the Germans in their holes while we sneak up on them.

The attacking squads sneak up the sides of the hedgerows while the rest of the platoon stay back in their own hedgerow and keep the forward hedge saturated with bullets. They shoot rifle grenades too, and a mortar squad a little farther back keeps lobbing mortar shells over onto the Germans.

The little advance groups get up to the far ends of the hedgerows at the corners of the field. They first try to knock out the machine guns at each corner. They do this with hand grenades, rifle grenades and machine guns.

Usually, when the pressure gets on, the German defenders of the hedgerow start pulling back. They'll take their heavier guns and most of the men back a couple of fields and start digging in for a new line.

They leave about two machine guns and a few riflemen scattered through the hedge, to do a lot of shooting and hold up the Americans as long as they can.

Our men now sneak along the front side of the hedgerow, throwing grenades over onto the other side and spraying the hedges with their guns. The fighting is very close - only a few yards apart - but it is seldom actual hand-to-hand stuff.

Sometimes the remaining Germans come out of their holes with their hands up. Sometimes they try to run for it and are mowed down. Sometimes they won't come out at all, and a hand grenade, thrown into their hole, finishes them off.

And so, we've taken another hedgerow and are ready to start on the one beyond.

This hedgerow business is a series of little skirmishes like that clear across the front, thousands and thousands of little skirmishes. No single one of them is very big. But add them all up over the days and weeks and you've got a man-sized war, with thousands on both sides being killed.

8/12/44
On the Western Front

What we gave you yesterday in trying to describe hedgerow fighting was the general pattern.

If you were to come over here and pick out some hedge-enclosed field at random, the fighting there probably wouldn't be following the general pattern at all. For each one is a little separate war, fought under different circumstances.

For instance, you'll come to a wood instead of an open field. The Germans will be dug in all over the woods, in little groups, and it's really tough to get them out. Often, in cases like that we will just go around the woods and keep going, and let later units take care of those surrounded and doomed fellows.

Or we'll go through the wood and clean it out, and another company, coming through a couple of hours later, will find it full of Germans again. In a war like this one everything is in such confusion, I don't see how either side ever got anywhere.

Sometimes, you don't know where the enemy is and don't know where your own troops are. As somebody said the other day, no battalion commander can give you the exact location of his various units five minutes after they've jumped off.

We will by-pass whole pockets of Germans, and they will be there fighting our following waves when our attacking companies are a couple of miles on beyond. Gradually, the front gets all mixed up. There will be Germans behind you and at the side. They'll be shooting at you from behind and from your flank.

Sometimes a unit will get so far out ahead of those on either side that it has to swing around and fight to its rear. Sometimes we fire on our own troops, thinking we are in German territory. You can't see anything, and you can't even tell from the sounds, for each side uses some of the other's captured weapons.

***

The tanks and the infantry had to work in the closest cooperation in breaking through the German ring that tried to pin us down in the beachhead area. Neither could have done it alone.

The troops are of two minds about having tanks around them. If you're a foot soldier, you hate to be near a tank, for it always draws fire. On the other hand, if the going gets tough, you pray for a tank to come up and start blasting with its guns.

In our breakthrough, each infantry unit had tanks attached to it. It was the tanks and the infantry that broke through, that ring and punched a hole for the armored divisions to go through.

The armored divisions practically ran amuck, racing long distances and playing hob, once they got behind the German lines, but it was the infantry and their attached tanks that opened the gate for them.

Tanks shuttled back and forth, from one field to another, throughout our breakthrough battle, receiving their orders by radio. Bulldozers punched holes through the hedgerows for them, and then the tanks would come up and blast out the bad spots of the opposition.

It has been necessary for us to wreck almost every farmhouse and little village in our path. The Germans used them for strong points, or put artillery observers in them, and they just had to be blasted out.

Most of the French farmers evacuate ahead of the fighting and filter back after it has passed. It is pitiful to see them come back to their demolished homes and towns. Yet, it's wonderful to see the grand way they take it.

***

In a long drive, an infantry company may go for a couple of days without letting up. Ammunition is carried up to it by hand, and occasionally by jeep. The soldiers sometimes eat only one K-ration a day. They may run clear out of water. Their strength is gradually whittled down by wounds, exhaustion cases and straggling.

Finally, they will get an order to sit where they are and dig in. Then another company will pass through, or around them, and go on with the fighting. The relieved company may get to rest as much as a day or two. But in a big push such as the one that broke us out of the beachhead, a few hours is about all they can expect.

The company I was with got its orders to rest about 5 one afternoon They dug foxholes along the hedgerows, or commandeered German ones already dug. Regardless of how tired you may be, you always dig in the first thing.

Then they sent some men with cans looking for water. They got more K-rations up by jeep and sat on the ground eating them[40].

They hoped they would stay there all night, but they weren't counting on it too much. Shortly after supper, a lieutenant came out of a farmhouse and told the sergeants to pass the

---

40. The K ration was a food ration comprised of breakfast, lunch and dinner.

word to be ready to move in 10 minutes. They bundled on their packs and started just before dark.

Within half an hour, they had run into a new fight that lasted all night. They had had less than four hours' rest in three solid days of fighting. That's the way life is in the infantry.

8/14/44
On the Western Front

The afternoon was tense and full of caution and dire little might-have-beens. I was wandering up a dirt lane where the infantrymen were squatting alongside in a ditch, waiting their turn to advance. They always squat like that when they're close to the front.

Suddenly, German shells started banging around us. I jumped into a ditch between a couple of soldiers and squatted. Shells were clipping the hedgetops right over our heads and crashing into the next pasture.

Then, suddenly, one exploded, not with a crash, but with a ring as though you'd struck a high-toned ball. The debris of burned wadding and dirt came showering down over us. My head rang and my right ear couldn't hear anything.

The shell had struck behind us, 20 feet away. We have been saved by the earthen bank of the hedgerow. It was the next day before my ear returned to normal. A minute later a soldier crouching next in line, a couple of feet away, turned to me and asked, 'Are you a war correspondent?'

I said I was, and he said, 'I want to shake your hand.' And he reached around the bush and we shook hands. That's all either of us did. It didn't occur to me until later that it was a sort of unusual experience. And I was so addled by the close explosions that I forgot to put down his name.

A few minutes later, a friend of mine, Lieut. Col. Oma Bates, of Gloster, Miss., came past and said he was hunting our new battalion command post. It was supposed to be in a farmhouse about a hundred yards from us, so I got up and went with him.

We couldn't find it at first. We lost about five minutes, walking around in orchards looking for it. That was a blessed five minutes For when we got within 50 yards of the house it got a direct

shell hit which killed one officer and wounded several men.

The Germans now rained shells around our little area. You couldn't walk 10 feet without hitting the ground. They came past our heads so quickly you didn't take time to fall forward - I found the quickest way down was to flop back and sideways.

In a little while, the seat of my pants was plastered thick with wet red clay, and my hands were scratched from hitting rocks and briars to break quick falls.

Nobody ever fastens the chin strap on his helmet in the front lines, for the blast from nearby bursts have been known to catch helmets and break people's necks. Consequently, when you squat quickly you descend faster than your helmet and you leave it in mid-air above you. Of course, in a fraction of a second, it follows you down and hits you on the head and settles sideways over your ear and down over your eyes. It makes you feel silly.

Once more, shells drove me into a roadside ditch. I squatted there, just a bewildered guy in brown, part of a thin line of other bewildered guys as far up and down the ditch as you could see.

It was really frightening. Our own shells were whanging overhead and hitting just beyond. The German shells tore through the orchards around us. There was machine-gunning all around, and bullets zipped through the trees above us.

I could tell by their shoulder patches that the soldiers near me were from a division to our right, and I wondered what they were doing there. Then I heard one of them say, 'This is a fine foul-up for you! I knew that lieutenant was getting lost. Hell, we're service troops, and here we are right in the front lines.'

Grim as the moment was, I had to laugh to myself at their pitiful plight.

I left a command post in a farmhouse and started to another about 10 minutes away. When I got there, they said the one I had just left had been hit white I was on the way.

A solid armor-piercing shell had gone right through a window, and a man I knew had his leg cut off. That evening the other officers took the big steel slug over to the hospital, so he would have a souvenir.

When I got to another battalion command post, later in the day, they were just ready to move. A sergeant had been forward about half a mile in a jeep and picked out a farmhouse. He said it was the cleanest, nicest one he had been in for a long time.

So, we piled into several jeeps and drove up there. It had been only about 20 minutes since the sergeant had left. But when we got to the new house, it wasn't there.

A shell had hit it in the fast 20 minutes and set it afire, and it had burned to the ground.

So, we drove up the road a little farther and picked out another one. We had been there about half an hour when a shell struck in an orchard 50 yards in front of us.

In a few minutes our litter bearers came past, carrying a captain. He was the surgeon of our adjoining battalion, and he had been looking in the orchard for a likely place to move his first-aid station. A shell hit right beside him.

That's the way war is on an afternoon that is tense and full of might-have-beens for some of us, and awful realities for others.

It just depends on what your number is. I don't believe in that number business at all, but in war you sort of let your belief hover around it, for it's about all you have left.

8/15/44
On the Western Front

One afternoon, I went with our battalion medics to pick up wounded men who had been carried back to some shattered houses just behind our lines, and to gather some others right off the battlefield.

The battalion surgeon was Capt. Lucien Strawn, from Morgantown, W. Va. He drives his jeep himself and goes right into the lines with his aidmen.

We drove forward about a mile in our two jeeps, so loaded with litter bearers they were even riding on the hood. Finally, we had to stop and wait until a bulldozer filled a new shell crater in the middle of the road. We had gone only about a hundred yards beyond the crater when we ran into some infantry. They stopped us and said, 'Be careful where you're going. The Germans are only 200 yards up the road.'

Captain Strawn said he couldn't get to the wounded men that way, so he turned around to try another way. A side road led off at an angle from a shattered village we had just passed through. He decided to try to get up that road.

But when we got there, the road had a house blown across it, and it was blocked. We went forward a little on foot and found two deep bomb craters, also impassable.

So, Captain Straw walked back to the bulldozer, and asked the driver if he would go ahead of us and clear the road. The first thing the driver asked was, 'How close to the front is it?'

The doctor said, 'Well, at least it isn't any closer than you right now.' So the dozer driver agreed to clear the road ahead of us.

While we were waiting, a soldier came over and showed us two eggs he had just found in the backyard of a jumbled house. There wasn't an untouched house left standing in the town, and some of the houses were still smoking inside.

Also, while we were waiting, two shock cases came staggering down the road toward us. They were not wounded but were completely broken – the kind that stab into your heart.

They were shaking all over and had to hold onto each other like little girls when they walked. The doctor stopped them. They could barely talk, barely understand. He told them to wait down at the next corner until we came back, and then they could ride.

When they turned away from the jeep, they turned slowly and unsteadily, a step at a time, like men who were awfully drunk.

Their mouths hung open and their eyes stared, and they still held onto each other. They were just like idiots. They had found more war than the spirit can endure.

At the far edge of the town, we came to a partly wrecked farmhouse that had two Germans in it - one was wounded and the other was just staying with him. We ran our jeeps into the yard and the litter bearers went on across the field to where the aid men had been told some of our wounded were lying behind a hedge.

The doctor sent the able German soldier along with our litter bearers to help carry. He was very willing to help. I stayed at house with the doctor while he looked at the wounded German, lying in the midst of the scattered debris of what had been a kitchen floor. The German didn't seem to be badly wounded, but he was sure full of misery. He looked middle-aged, and he was pale, partly bald, had a big nose and his face was yellow. He kept moaning and twisting. The doctor said he thought morphine was making him sick.

The doctor took his scissors and began cutting his clothes open to see if he was wounded anywhere except in the arm. But he had been sick at his stomach and then rolled over. He was sure a superman sad sack.

Pretty soon the litter bearers came back. They had two wounded Germans and one American on their litters. Also, they had two walking cases - one hearty fellow with a slight leg wound, and one youngster whose hands were trembling from nervous tension.

The doctor asked him what was the matter and he said nothing was, except he couldn't stop shaking. He said he felt that his nerves were all right, but he just couldn't keep his hands from trembling.

He was a machine gunner on a half-track. Captain Strawn talked kindly to him.

'Who sent you back?' he asked.

'We've got a new lieutenant,' the boy said, 'and he told me to come back and report to an aid station for rest.'

The doctor thought a while. 'I can't send you to a hospital,' the doctor said. 'You're not in very bad shape and they need men too badly up there.'

Just a shade of disappointment passed over the boy's face, but he was game.

'That's what I told the lieutenant,' he said. 'I think I'm all right to go back.'

I could tell the doctor liked his attitude. There was nothing yellow about the kid.

The doctor said, 'I'll tell you. You get on this jeep and go back to the aid station. We will give you some sleeping stuff, and you can just lie around there on the ground for a day or two and you'll be all right.'

And with that compromise the kid - relieved at even a two-day respite - got into the jeep with the wounded men and went back down the road.

8/16/44
On the Western Front

The other soldier had a white bandage around the calf of his left leg. He had loosely laced his legging back over the bandage.

He said the wound 'didn't amount to a damn' and he wished they hadn't sent him back from the lines. He said he had gone through Africa and Sicily without getting wounded, and now he'd got nicked. He was disgusted.

You could sense that this guy was a fine soldier. He looked old, but probably wasn't. I took him to be a farmer. He talked like a hillbilly, and beneath his whiskers you could tell he had a big, droll face.

He had found some long, crooked, raggedy French cigars, and he kept lighting these funny-looking things and putting them about three inches into his mouth. He wasn't nervous in the least.

Capt. Lucien Strawn, the battalion surgeon, started to put him in a jeep to go back to the aid station, but the soldier said, 'Now wait. I know where there's two more men wounded pretty bad. One of them is a lieutenant who just got back from the hospital this morning from his other wound.'

The soldier said they were right up where the bullets were flying, but that if the aidmen would go he could walk well enough to guide them up there. So, the doctor named off half a dozen men to go with him.

The doctor also said the unwounded German to go along and help carry. But one of the aidmen said, 'We better not have him with us. Our own men are liable to start shooting at us.'

'That's right,' the doctor said, 'leave him here.' And he named off one other American to go. After they had left the doctor said, 'That's the truth, and I never even thought of it.'

The doctor and I sat a while on the stairway inside the farmhouse for shells had started hitting just outside again. But in a little bit, the doctor got up and said he was going to see how the stretcher party was getting along. I said, I'd like to go with him. He said OK.

We struck out across a sloping wheatfield. It was full of huge craters left by our bombings. There was a lull in the shelling as we crossed the field, but the trouble with lulls is that you never know when they will suddenly come to an end.

As we picked our way among the craters I thought I heard, very faintly, somebody call, 'Help!' It's odd how things strike you in wartime. I remember thinking to myself, 'Oh, pooh, that would be too dramatic - just like a book. You're just imagining it.'

But the doctor had stopped, and he said, 'Did you hear somebody yelling?'

So, we listened again, and this time we could hear it plainly. It seemed to come from a far corner of the field, so we picked our way over in that direction.

Finally, we saw him, a soldier lying on his back near a hedgerow, still yelling, 'Help!' as we approached. The aidmen who had started ahead of us had got down in a bomb crater when the shelling started, so the doctor now waved them to come on.

The wounded soldier was making an awful fuss. He was twisting and squirming, and moaning, 'Oh, my God! Oh, my God!'

He had a bandage on his right hand and there was blood on his left leg.

The doctor took his scissors and cut the legging off, then cut the laces on the shoe, and then peeled off a bloody sock and cut the pants leg up so he could see the wound. The soldier kept his eyes shut and kept squirming and moaning.

When the doctor would try to talk to him, he would just groan and say, 'Oh, my God!' Finally, the doctor got out of him that he had had a small wound in his hand, and his sergeant had bandaged it and told him to start to the rear. Then, coming across the field, a shell fragment had got him in the leg.

The doctor looked him over thoroughly. There were two small holes just above the ankle. The doctor said they hadn't touched the bone. I think the doctor was disgusted.

He said, 'He's making a hell of a fuss over nothing.' Then to one of the aidmen he said, 'Better give him a shot of morphine to quiet him.'

Whereupon the soldier squirmed and moaned, 'Oh, no, no, no! Oh, my God!' But the doctor said go ahead, and the aidman cut his sleeve up to the shoulder, stuck the needle in and squeezed the vial.

The aidman, trying to be sympathetic said to the soldier, 'It's the same old needle, ain't it?' But the soldier just groaned again and said, 'Oh, my God!'

Our hillbilly soldier lit another skinny cigar, as though he were at a national convention instead of a battlefield. Then one set of the litterbearers started back with our new man, and the rest of us went on with the soldier to hunt for other wounded.

8/17/44
On the Western Front

The commander of the particular regiment of the 4th Infantry Division that we have been with is one of my favorites.

That's partly because he flatters me by calling me 'General', partly because just looking at him makes me chuckle to myself, and partly because I think he's a very fine soldier.

Security forbids my giving his name. He is a Regular Army colonel and he was overseas in the last war. His division commander says the only trouble with him is that he's too bold, and if he isn't careful, he's liable to get clipped one of these days.

He is rather unusual looking. There is something almost Mongolian about his face. When cleaned up he could be a Cossack. When tired and dirty he could be a movie gangster. But either way, his eyes always twinkle.

He has a facility for direct thought that is unusual. He is impatient of thinking that gets off onto byways.

He has a little habit of good-naturedly reprimanding people by cocking his head over to one side, getting his face below yours and saying something sharp, and then looking up at you with a quizzical smirk like a laughing cat.

One day, I heard him ask a battalion commander what his position was. The battalion commander started going into details of why his troops hadn't got as far as he had hoped. The colonel cocked his head over, squinted up at the battalion commander, and said, 'I didn't ask you that. I asked you where you were.'

The colonel goes constantly from one battalion to another during battle, from early light till darkness. He wears a new-type field jacket that fits him like a sack, and he carries a long stick that Teddy Roosevelt[41] gave him. He keeps constantly prodding his commanders to push hard not to let up, to keep driving and driving.

He is impatient with commanders who lose the main point of the war by getting involved in details - the main point, of course, being to kill Germans. His philosophy of war is expressed in the simple formula of 'shoot the sonsabitches.'

Once I was at a battalion command post when we got word that 60 Germans were coming down the road in a counterattack. Everybody got excited. They called the colonel on a field phone, gave him the details and asked him what to do. He had the solution in a nutshell. He just said, 'Shoot the sonsabitches' and hung up.

Another of my favorites is a sergeant who runs the colonel's regimental mess. He cooks some himself, but mostly he bosses the cooking.

His name is Charles J, Murphy and his home is at (225 East State St.) Trenton N.J. Murph is redheaded, but has his head nearly shaved like practically all the western front soldiers - officers as well as men. Murph is funny, but he seldom smiles.

When I asked him what he did in civilian life, he thought a moment and then said, 'Well, I was a shyster. Guess you'd call me a kind of promoter. I always had the kind of job where you made $50 a week salary and $1,500 on the side.'

---

41. Second in Command of the U.S. 4th Infantry Division, Teddy Roosevelt died of a heart attack on 12 July 1944, in Méautis, in Manche.

How's that for an honest man?

Murph and I got to talking about newspapermen one day. Murph said his grandfather was a newspaperman. He retired in old age and lived in Murph's house.

'My grandfather went nuts reading newspapers,' Murph said. 'It was a phobia with him. Every day, he'd buy $1.50 worth of 3-cent newspapers and then read them all night. He wouldn't read the ads. He would just read the stories, looking for something to criticize. He'd get fuming mad. Lots of times when I was a kid he'd get me out of bed at 2 or 3 in the morning and point to some story in the paper and rave about reporters who didn't have sense enough to put a period at the end of a sentence.'

Murph and I agreed that it was fortunate his grandfather passed on before he got to reading my stuff, or he would doubtless have run amuck.

Murph never smoked cigarets until he landed in France on D-Day, but now he smokes one after another. He is about the tenth soldier who has told me that same thing. A guy in war has to have some outlet for his nerves, and I guess smoking is as good as anything.

All kinds of incongruous things happen during a battle. For instance, during one lull I got my portrait painted in watercolor. The artist sat crosslegged on the grass and it took about an hour.

The painter was Pfc. Leon Wall, from Wyoming, Pa. He went to the National Academy of Design in New York for six years, did research for the Metropolitan Museum and lectured on art at the New York World's Fair.

Artist Wall is now of all things a cook and KP in an infantry regiment mess. He hasn't done any war paintings at all since the invasion. I asked him why not. He said, 'Well, at first I was too scared, and since then I've been too busy.'

8/18/44
On the Western Front

Soldiers are made out of the strangest people.

I've recently made a new friend - just a plain old Hoosier[42] - who is so quiet and humble you would hardly know he was around. Yet in our few weeks of invasion, he has killed four of the enemy, and he has learned war's wise little ways of destroying life and preserving your own.

He hasn't become the 'killer' type that war makes of some soldiers; he has merely become adjusted to an obligatory new profession. His name is George Thomas Clayton. Back home he is known as Tommy. In the Army he is sometimes called George, but usually just Clayton. He is from Evansville, where he lived with his sister (at 862 Covart Ave.). He is a front-line infantryman of a rifle company in the 29th Division.

By the time this is printed, he will be back in the lines. Right now, he is out of combat for a brief rest. He spent a few days in an 'Exhaustion Camp', then was assigned briefly to the camp where I work from - a camp for correspondents. That's how we got acquainted.

Clayton is a private first class. He operates a Browning automatic rifle. He has turned down two chances to become a buck sergeant and squad leader, simply because he would

---

42. *Originating from Indiana, just like Ernie Pyle himself.*

rather keep his powerful B.A.R. than have stripes and less personal protection.

He landed in Normandy on D-Day, on the toughest of the beaches[43], and was in the line for 37 days without rest. He has had innumerable narrow escapes.

Twice, 88s hit within a couple of arms' lengths of him. But both times the funnel of the concussion was away from him and he didn't get a scratch, though the explosions covered him and his rifle with dirt.

Then a third one hit about 10 feet away and made him deaf in his right ear. He had always had trouble with that ear anyway - ear aches and things as a child. Even in the Army back in America he had to beg the doctors to waive the ear defect in order to come overseas. He is still a little hard of hearing in that ear from the shell burst, but it's gradually coming back.

When Tommy finally left the lines he was pretty well done up and his sergeant wanted to send him to a hospital but he begged not to go for fear he wouldn't get back to his old company, so they let him go to a rest camp instead.

And now, after a couple of weeks with us (provided the correspondents don't drive him frantic), he will return to the lines with his old outfit.

Clayton has worked at all kinds of things back in that other world of civilian life. He has been a farm hand, a cook and a bartender. Just before he joined the Army, he was a gauge-honer in the Chrysler Ordnance Plant at Evansville.

---

43. *The 29th Division was among the first waves of assault on Omaha Beach on 6 June 1944.*

When the war is over, he wants to go into business for himself for the first time in his life. He'll probably set up a small restaurant in Evansville. He said his brother-in-law would back him.

Tommy was shipped overseas after only two months in the Army, and now has been out of America for 18 months. He is medium-sized, dark-haired, has a little mustache and the funniest-looking head of hair you ever saw this side of Buffalo Bill's show.

While his division was killing time in the last few days before leaving England, he and three others decided to have their hair cut Indian fashion. They had their heads clipped down to the skin except a two-inch ridge starting at the forehead and running clear to the back of the neck. It makes them look more comical than ferocious, as they had intended. Two of the four have been wounded and evacuated to England.

I chatted off and on with Clayton for several days before he told me how old he was. I was amazed; so much so that I asked several other people to guess at his age and they all guessed about the same as I did - about 26.

Actually, he is 37, and that's pretty well along in years to be a front-line infantryman. It's harder on a man at that age.

As Clayton himself says, 'When you pass that 30 mark you begin to slow up a little.'

It's harder for you to take the hard ground and the rain and the sleeplessness and the unending wracking of it all. And yet at 37 he elected to go back.

(More tomorrow)

8/19/44
On the Western Front

The ways of an invasion turned out to be all very new to Pfc. Tommy Clayton, the 29th division infantryman we were writing about yesterday.

It was new to thousands of others also, for they hadn't been trained in hedgerow fighting. So, they had to learn it the way a dog learns to swim. They learned.

As we said yesterday, this Tommy Clayton, the mildest of men, has killed four of the enemy for sure, and probably dozens of unseen ones. He wears an Expert Rifleman's badge and soon will have the proud badge of Combat Infantryman, worn only by those who have been through the mill.

Three of his four victims he got in one long blast of his Browning automatic rifle. He was stationed in the bushes at a bend in a gravel road, covering a crossroads about 80 yards ahead of him.

Suddenly, three German soldiers came out a side road and foolishly stopped to talk right in the middle of the crossroads. The B.A.R. has 20 bullets in a clip. Clayton held her down for the whole clip. The three Germans went down, never to get up.

His fourth one he thought was a Jap when he killed him. In the early days of the invasion, lots of soldiers thought they were fighting Japs, scattered in with the German troops. They were actually Mongolian Russians, with strong Oriental features, who resembled Japs to the untraveled Americans.

On this fourth killing, Clayton was covering an infantry squad as it worked forward along a hedgerow. There were snipers in the trees in front. Clayton spotted one and sprayed the tree with his automatic rifle, and out tumbled this man he thought was a Jap.

To show how little anyone who hasn't been through war can know about it - do you want to know how Clayton located his sniper?

Here's how.

When a bullet passes smack over your head it doesn't zing; it pops the same as a rifle when it goes off. That's because the bullet's rapid passage creates a vacuum behind it, and the air rushes back with such force to fill this vacuum that it collides with itself and makes a resounding 'pop'.

Clayton didn't know what caused this, and I tried to explain. 'You know what a vacuum is,' I said. 'We learned that in high school.'

And Tommy said, 'Ernie, I never went past the third grade.'

But Tommy is intelligent and his sensitivities are fine. You don't have to know the reasons in war, you only have to know what things indicate when they happen.

Well, Clayton had learned that the pop of a bullet over his head preceded the actual rifle report by a fraction of a second, because the sound of the rifle explosion had to travel some distance before hitting his ear. So, the 'pop' became his warning signal to listen for the crack of a sniper's rifle a moment later.

Through much practice, he had learned to gauge the direction of the sound almost exactly. And so out of this animal-like system of hunting, he had the knowledge to shoot into the right tree - and out tumbled his 'Jap' sniper.

Clayton's weirdest experience would be funny if it weren't so flooded with pathos. He was returning with a patrol one moonlit night when the enemy opened up on them. Tommy leaped right through a hedge and, spotting a foxhole, plunged into it.

To his amazement and fright, there was a German in the foxhole, sitting pretty, holding a machine pistol in his hands.

Clayton shot him three times in the chest before you could say scat.

The German hardly moved. And then Tommy realized the man had been killed earlier. He had been shooting a corpse.

All these experiences seem to have left no effect on this mild soldier from Indiana, unless to make him even quieter than before. The worst experience of all is just the accumulated blur, and the hurting vagueness of too long in the lines, the everlasting alertness, the noise and fear, the cell-by-cell exhaustion, the thinning of the ranks around you as day follows nameless day. And the constant march into eternity of your own small quota of chances for survival.

Those are the things that hurt and destroy. And soldiers like Tommy Clayton go back to them, because they are good soldiers, and they have a duty they cannot define.

8/21/44
On the Western Front

When you're wandering around our very far-flung front lines - the lines that in our present rapid war are known as 'fluid' - you can always tell how recently the battle has swept on ahead of you.

You can sense it from the little things even more than the big things.

From the scattered green leaves and the fresh branches of trees still lying in the middle of the road.

From the wisps and coils of telephone wire, hanging brokenly from high poles and entwining across the roads.

From the gray, burned-powder rims of the shell craters in the gravel roads, their edges not yet smoothed by the pounding of military traffic.

From the little pools of blood on the roadside, blood that has only begun to congeal and turn black, and the punctured steel helmets lying nearby.

From the square blocks of building stone still scattered in the village streets, and from the sharp-edged rocks in the roads, still uncrushed by traffic.

From the burned-out tanks and broken carts still unremoved from the road. From the cows in the fields, lying grotesquely with their feet to the sky, so newly dead they have not begun to bloat or smell.

From the scattered heaps of personal debris around a gun. I don't know why it is, but the Germans always seem to take off their coats before they flee or die.

From all those things, you can tell that the battle has been recent - from these and from the men dead so recently that they seem to be merely asleep.

And, also, from the inhuman quiet. Usually, battles are noisy for miles around. But in this recent fast warfare, a battle sometimes leaves a complete vacuum behind it.

The Germans will stand and fight it out until they see there is no hope. Then some give up, and the rest pull and run for miles. Shooting stops. Our fighters move on after the enemy, and those who do not fight, but move in the wake of the battles will not catch up for hours.

There is nothing left behind but the remains - the lifeless debris, the sunshine and the flowers, and utter silence. An amateur who wanders in this vacuum at the rear of a battle has a terrible sense of loneliness. Everything is dead - the men, the machines, the animals - and you alone are left alive.

One afternoon we drove in our jeep into a country like that. The little rural villages of gray stone were demolished - heartbreaking heaps of still smoking rubble.

We drove into the tiny town of La Detinais, a sweet old stone village at the 'T' of two gravel roads, a rural village in rolling country, a village of not more than 50 buildings. There was not a whole building left.

Rubble and broken wires still littered the streets. Blackish gray-stone walls with no roofs still smoldered inside. Dead men still lay in the street, helmets and broken rifles askew around them. There was not a soul nor a sound in town; the village was lifeless.

We stopped and pondered our way, and with trepidation we drove on out of town. We drove for a quarter of a mile or so. The ditches were full of dead men. We drove around one without a head or arms or legs. We stared, and couldn't say anything about it to each other.

We asked the driver to go very slowly, for there was an uncertainty in all the silence. There was no live human, no sign of movement anywhere.

Seeing no one, hearing nothing, I became fearful of going on into the unknown. So, we stopped. Just a few feet ahead of us was a brick-red American tank, still smoking, and with its turret knocked off. Near it was a German horse-drawn ammunition cart, upside down. In the road beside them was a shell crater.

To our left lay two smashed airplanes in adjoining fields. Neither of them was more than 30 yards from the road. The hedge was low and we could see over. They were both British fighter planes, One lay right side up, the other lay on its back.

We were just ready to turn around and go back, when I spied a lone soldier at the far side of the field. He was standing there looking across the field at us like an Indian in a picture. I waved and he waved back. We walked toward each other.

He turned out to be a second lieutenant - Ed Sasson, of (8137 Mulholland Terrace) Los Angeles, He is a graves registration officer for his armored division, and he was out scouring the fields, locating the bodies of dead Americans.

He was glad to see somebody, for it is a lonely job catering to the dead.

As we stood there talking in the lonely field, a soldier in coveralls with a rifle slung over his shoulder ran up breathlessly, and almost shouted, 'Hey there's a man alive in one of those planes across the road. He's been trapped there for days!'

We stopped right in the middle of a sentence and began to run. We hopped the hedgerow, and ducked under the wing of the upside-down plane. And there, in the next hour, came the climax to what certainly was one of the really great demonstrations of courage in this war.

8/22/44
On the Western Front

We ran to the wrecked British plane, lying there upside down, and dropped on our hands and knees and peeked through a tiny hole in the side.

A man lay on his back in the small space of the upside-down cockpit. His feet disappeared somewhere in the jumble of dials and rubber pedals above him. His shirt was open and his chest was bare to the waist. He was smoking a cigaret.

He turned his eyes toward me when I peeked in, and he said in a typical British manner of offhand friendliness, 'Oh, hello.'

'Are you all right,' I asked, stupidly.

He answered, 'Yes, quite. Now that you chaps are here!'

I asked him how long he had been trapped in the wrecked plane.

He said he didn't know for sure as he had got mixed up about the passage of time. But he did know the date of the month he was shot down. He told me the date. And I said out loud, 'Good God!'

For, wounded and trapped, he had been lying there for eight days!

His left leg was broken and punctured by an ack-ack burst. His back was terribly burned by raw gasoline that had spilled.

The foot of his injured leg was pinned rigidly under the rudder bar.

His space was so small he couldn't squirm around to relieve his own weight from his paining back. He couldn't straighten out his legs, which were bent above him. He couldn't see out of his little prison. He had not had a bite to eat or a drop of water. All this for eight days and nights.

Yet when we found him, his physical condition was strong, and his mind was as calm and rational as though he were sitting in a London club. He was in agony, yet in his correct Oxford accent he even apologized for taking up our time to get him out.

The American soldiers of our rescue party cussed as they worked, cussed with open admiration for this British flier's greatness of heart which had kept him alive and sane through his lonely and gradually hope-dimming ordeal.

One of them said, 'God, but these Limies[44] have got guts!'

It took us almost an hour to get him out. We don't know whether he will live or not, but he has a chance. During the hour we were ripping the plane open to make a hole, he talked to us. And here, in the best nutshell I can devise from the conversation of a brave man whom you didn't want to badger with trivial questions is what happened.

---

44. *The term 'Limies' used by Ernie Pyle is a colloquialism first mentioned in the 19th century in the United States and referring to the British sailors who had developed the habit of sucking lemons to prevent the onset of scurvy. By extension, the term tended to refer to all British troops.*

He was an RAF flight lieutenant, piloting a night fighter. Over a certain area the Germans began letting him have it from the ground with machine-gun fire.

The first hit knocked out his motor. He was too low to jump, so - foolishly, he said - he turned on his lights to try a crash landing Then they really poured it on him. The second hit got him in the leg. And a third bullet cut right across the balls of his right-hand forefingers, clipping every one of them to the bone.

He left his wheels up, and the plane's belly hit the ground going uphill on a slight slope. We could see the groove it had dug for about 50 yards. Then it flopped, tail over nose, onto its back.

The pilot was absolutely sealed into the upside-down cockpit.

'That's all I remember for a while,' he told us. 'When I came to, they were shelling all around me.'

Thus began the eight days. He had crashed right between the Germans and Americans in a sort of pastoral no-man's land.

For days afterwards the field in which he lay surged back and forth between German hands and ours. His pasture was pocked with hundreds of shell craters. Many of them were only yards away. One was right at the end of his wing. The metal sides of the plane were speckled with hundreds of shrapnel holes.

He lay there, trapped in the midst of this inferno of explosions. The fields around him gradually became littered with dead. At last, American strength pushed the Germans back, and silence came. But no help. Because, you see, it was in that vacuum behind the battle, and only a few people were left.

The days passed. He thirsted terribly. He slept some; part of the time he was unconscious; part of the time he undoubtedly was delirious. But he never gave up hope.

After we had finally got him out, he said as he lay on the stretcher under a wing, 'Is it possible that I've been out of this plane since I crashed?'

Everybody chuckled. The doctor who had arrived said, 'Not the remotest possibility. You were sealed in there and it took men with tools half an hour to make an opening. And your leg was broken and your foot was pinned there. No, you haven't been out.'

'I didn't think it was possible,' the pilot said, 'and yet it seems in my mind that I was out once and back in again.'

That little memory of delirium was the only word said by that remarkable man in the whole hour of his rescue that wasn't as dispassionate and matter-of-fact as though he had been sitting comfortably at the end of the day in front of his own fireplace.

8/22/44
On the Western Front

I would like to tell you in detail the remarkable story of the wounded RAF pilot whom we released after he had lain unnoticed in the wreckage of his plane for eight days on a battlefield.

Several American soldiers sprung out of somewhere a few moments after we arrived. They grasped the situation instantly and began tearing at the sides of the plane with pliers and wire clippers. They worked as though seconds had suddenly become jewels.

The tough metal came off in strips no bigger than your fingers, and only after terrific pulling and yanking. It seemed as if it would take hours to make a hole big enough to get the pilot out.

The ripping and pounding against the metal sides of the hollow plane made a thunderous noise. I peered inside and asked the pilot, 'Does the noise bother you?'

He said, 'No I can stand it. But tell them to be careful when they break through on the other side - my leg is broken, you know.'

But the American boys worked faster than we believed possible. They tore their fingers on the jagged edges of the metal; they broke strong aluminum ribs with one small crowbar and a lot of human strength. Soon they had a hole big enough so that I could get my head and shoulders inside the cockpit.

Somebody handed me a canteen of water and I shoved it through the hole to the pilot. He drank avidly. When he put the canteen down, he set it on his bare chest and held it with both hands.

'By God, I could drink a river dry,' he said.

Somebody outside said not to let him drink any more right now. The pilot said, 'Would you pour some on my head?'

I soaked my dirty handkerchief and rubbed his forehead with it. His hair was nut brown in color and very long. His whiskers were reddish and scraggly and he had a little mustache. His face seemed long and thin, and yet you could tell by his tremendous chest that he was a big man and powerful.

His eyes were not glassy, but I was fascinated by his eyeballs. They didn't protrude; it was just that they were so big. When he turned them toward you, it was as though he was slowly turning two big brown tennis balls.

He had complete command of his thoughts. The half-delirium you would expect of a man trapped for eight days without food or water just did not exist in him. He was just being himself.

His face was dirty from much sweating, but the skin of his body was white and clean. There was a small scab on his forehead and there were some light bruises on his arms.

Inside the plane, the stench was shocking. My first thought was that there must be another man in the plane who had been dead for days. I said to the pilot, 'Is there someone else in the plane?'

And he answered, "No, this is a single seater, old boy."

What I had smelled was the pilot himself. We couldn't see the lower part of his left leg, but we judged it must be gangrenous and in a horrible shape.

'I can move my right leg,' he said, 'it's all right. In fact, I've had it out from here several times, and moved it around for exercise. But the left one I can't move.'

I asked, 'Where did you get the cigaret you were smoking when we got here?'

He said, 'Your chap gave it to me. The one who came first. He lighted it for me and stuck it in through the hole, and went searching for the rest of you.'

I was wondering if it wasn't dangerous for him to be smoking inside the wrecked plane. I mentioned something about his being lucky that the plane hadn't caught fire when he crashed. And he said, 'I'll tell you about that. Do you see that woods a little way north of us?'

There were several small woods but I said, 'Yes.'

'Well,' he said, 'that first night they set fire to that woods. I could tell it by the glow in the cockpit. And here the plane was soaked with hundred-octane gasoline. I thought the fire would spread right across the field. But it didn't.'

Actually, what he had thought was the woods afire was the little town of La Detinais, which had been set afire by shelling. I didn't bother to tell him, for he was alive, and after all what could the technicalities matter?

8/23/44
On the Western Front

We had sent one soldier to the nearest aid station as soon as we discovered the wounded British pilot, trapped for eight days in his plane. He had to drive about six miles.

Just a few minutes after the other soldiers finished tearing two holes in the sides of the plane, a medical captain and three aidmen popped through the hedge and came running.

The doctor knelt down and sized up everything in a few seconds He asked an aidman for morphine. The pilot willingly held out his right arm, and the doctor stuck a needle into the bend of the elbow. The pilot never flinched, but looked on almost approvingly.

'You're in good condition,' the doctor said to him. 'This is just to make it easier for you when we start to pull you out. We'll wait a few minutes for it to take hold.'

While we were sitting there on the ground beside the plane, waiting for the morphine to take effect, the pilot said, 'I am delaying you from your work. I'm frightfully sorry about it.'

One of the soldiers, touched by the remark, blurted, 'Good God, leftenant, you aren't delaying us. This is what we're here for. We're just sorry we've been so long getting you out.'

The pilot momentarily closed his eyes and put his hand on his forehead. And then, as if in resignation at his own rudeness in bothering us, he said, 'Well, I don't know what I should do without you.'

So incredibly strong was that pilot's constitution that the morphine never put him out.

They waited about 10 minutes. Then two soldiers took off their web belts and looped them around the pilot's armpits. The medics on the other side said they had hold of his trapped foot and could gradually free it.

'It's my back that's weak,' the pilot said. 'All the strength seems to be gone from the small of my back. You'll have to help me there.'

They pulled. The pilot although without food for eight days, was tremendously strong, and he reached above his head to the plane's framework and helped lift himself.

The belts slipped, and the soldiers took them off. They knelt and lifted his shoulders with their hands.

They had padded the jagged edges of the torn aluminum, over which they would have to slide him, with the heavy rubber of his collapsible lifeboat.

The doctor said, 'We'll be as easy as we can. Tell us when to quit.' And the brave man said, 'Go ahead. I'll stand it as long as I can.'

They pulled again. The pilot made a face and exerted himself to help them. They slid him slowly a few inches through the hole, until he suddenly called, 'Whoa-whoa-whoa-whoa! My back! It's stuck to the ground. We'll have to break it loose slowly.'

They surveyed the possibilities a while, trying to figure a less painful way of getting him out. There wasn't any. He said, 'I can't raise my behind at all. If you could slide something under me to carry the weight.'

A soldier went running to the next field, looking for a board. We waited. In a few minutes, he came back with a short, thick board. The pilot reached up with his strong arms, made a face, and lifted himself a little from the ground, and the doctor slid the board underneath him. Then the doctor, still kneeling, lifted one end of the board.

Gradually the pilot came out. Twice he had to stop them while they rearranged his injured leg. He said it was twisted. But apparently it was largely the agony of suddenly straightening out a cramped knee that had lain bent for eight days.

At last, in a sort of final surge, he came clear of the plane. They crawled backwards with him, on hands and knees, struggling to hold his back off the ground. You could see that he was steeling himself fiercely.

'Quick! Slide that litter under him,' the doctor called. The pilot said, 'My God, that air! That fresh air!' Three times in the next five minutes he mentioned the fresh air.

When they finally laid him tenderly onto the canvas litter and straightened his left leg, you could see the tendons relax and his facial muscles subside, and he gave a long half-groan, half-sigh of relief.

And that was the one single sound of normal human weakness uttered by that man of great courage in the hour of his liberation.

8/25/44
On the Western Front

You may have wondered how that British pilot happened to be found after lying for eight days unnoticed, trapped in his wrecked plane.

Well, as I told you, a bullet had clipped the balls of his right-hand forefingers, clear to the bone. He had put his cream-colored handkerchief over them to stop the bleeding. As the wound dried, the handkerchief stuck to his fingers, and to pull it off would have been painful. It still stuck to his fingers all through the ordeal of getting him out; it was still clasped in his hand as the ambulance jeep drove away with him.

To go back, through the days of his waiting he had that handkerchiefed right hand stuck through a little hole in the plane's side, moving it slowly back and forth.

Just after I had stopped that day to talk to Lieut. Ed Sasson in the field, two mechanics from an armored division came down the road in a jeep. They were looking at the wrecked plane as they drove along, and suddenly they saw this slight movement. They stopped and went over to make sure, and they found inside there one of the brave men of this war. That's when they came running for us.

The two boys to whom this British flight lieutenant owes his life are Sergt. Milton Van Sickel, of Brainard, Minn., and Corp. William Schinke, of Gresham, Neb.

At last, we had the pilot out of the plane and on a stretcher under the wing. The doctor took some scissors and started cutting away his clothes. It must be hot in those cockpits in flight, for the pilot wore nothing but short trousers and a blue shirt.

The doctor cut off the pants and then the shirt. The pilot lay there naked. He was a man of magnificent physique.

The calves of his legs were large and athletic. In the calf of the left leg was a round hole as big as an apple. But to our astonishment there was no deterioration of flesh around it. The wound was already healing perfectly. The leg wasn't even burned, as he had told us. What then could it have been that we smelled in the plane?

We turned him over and then we saw. His back was burned by spilled gasoline, from his shoulders to the end of his spine. It was raw and red.

He had been forced to lie on it all the time, unable to move. At least, festering had started, and then gangrene. We could see the little blue-green mouldy splotches. That was what we had smelled.

He didn't know about that. The odor had developed inside his little cubbyhole so gradually that he hadn't been aware of it.

He was shocked by the smell of fresh air, but he still didn't know about the other. He had been worried only about his leg.

I don't know what the doctor really thought. The pilot was obviously in wonderful physical shape, considering such an ordeal. The doctor told him so. But he looked a long time at that gangrenous back, and then, they temporarily bandaged it.

As they were working on him, the doctor asked if the pilot had a wallet or any papers. He said yes, his had been in his hip pocket. The doctor lifted the blood-smeared pants and cut the wallet out, with a pair of scissors. From the other pocket he cut a silver cigaret case.

'That's good, old boy,' the pilot said. 'I'm grateful that you found that.'

We asked him if he had a wristwatch. He said yes, but it had fallen off and was probably in the debris where he had been lying. But we couldn't find it, and finally gave it up.

As he lay on his stomach on the stretcher, they tied a metal splint around his wounded leg. While they were doing this, I bathed his head again in water from a canteen.

A soldier lit another cigaret and gave it to him. It dropped through his fingers onto the wet grass, and became soaked. I lit another one and put it in his fingers.

He took a long, deep drag, and put his head down on the litter and closed his eyes. The morphine finally was making him groggy, but it never did put him out.

The cigaret burned up almost to his fingers. An officer said, 'It's going to burn him,' and started to pull it from between his fingers. But the pilot heard and lazily opened his eyes, took another puff and with his thumb pushed the cigaret farther out in his fingers Then he closed his eyes again. He lay there for a few minutes like that.

Then again, he rolled those great eyes up and said to me, 'What date did you say this was?' I told him.

'That's wonderful,' he said. 'My wedding anniversary is just three days away. I guess I'll be back in England for it yet.'

He wouldn't, but everybody said, sure, maybe you will.

The medics were all through. They covered the naked pilot with a blanket and carried him to the road. Everybody in our little crowd loved the man who had the heart to be so wonderful.

As they put the stretcher down in the gravel road, waiting for the jeep to turn around, one of the armored division soldiers leaned over the stretcher and said with rough emotion, 'If you'd been a goddam German you'da been dead five days ago, Christ, but you British have got guts!'

8/28/44
Paris

I had thought that for me there could never again be any elation in war. But I had reckoned without the liberation of Paris - I had reckoned without remembering that I might be a part of this richly historic day.

We are in Paris - on the first day - one of the great days of all time. This is being written, as other correspondents are writing their pieces under an emotional tension, a pent-up semi-delirium.

Our approach to Paris was hectic. We had waited for three days in a nearby town while hourly our reports on what was going on in Paris changed and contradicted themselves. Of a morning it would look as though we were about to break through the German ring around Paris and come to the aid of the brave French Forces of the Interior who were holding parts of the city. By afternoon, it would seem the enemy had reinforced until another Stalingrad was developing. We could not bear to think of the destruction of Paris, and yet at times it seemed desperately inevitable.

That was the situation this morning when we left Rambouillet[45] and decided to feel our way timidly toward the very outskirts of Paris. And then, when we were within about eight miles, rumors began to circulate that the French Second Armored Division was in the city. We argued for half an hour at a crossroads with a French captain who was holding us up, and finally he freed us and waved us on.

For 15 minutes, we drove through a flat gardenlike country under a magnificent bright sun and amidst greenery, with distant banks of smoke pillaring the horizon ahead and to our left. And then we came gradually into the suburbs, and soon into Paris itself and a pandemonium of surely the greatest mass joy that has ever happened.

The streets were lined as by Fourth of July parade crowds at home, only this crowd was almost hysterical. The streets of Paris are very wide, and they were packed on each side. The women were all brightly dressed in white or red blouses and colorful peasant skirts, with flowers in their hair and big flashy earrings. Everybody was throwing flowers, and even serpentine.

---

45. *Southwest of Paris.*

As our jeep eased through the crowds, thousands of people crowded up, leaving only a narrow corridor, and frantic men, women and children grabbed us and kissed us and shook our hands and beat on our shoulders and slapped our backs and shouted their joy as we passed.

I was in a jeep with Henry Gorrell of the United Press, Capt. Carl Pergler of Washington, D. C. and Corp. Alexander Belon of Amherst, Mass. We all got kissed until we were literally red in face, and I must say we enjoyed it.

Once when the jeep was simply swamped in human traffic and had to stop, we were swarmed over and hugged and kissed and torn at. Everybody, even beautiful girls, insisted on kissing you on both cheeks. Somehow, I got started kissing babies that were held up by their parents, and for a while it looked like a baby-kissing politician going down the street. The fact that I hadn't shaved for days, and was graybearded as well as baldheaded, made no difference. Once, when we came to a stop, some Frenchmen told us there were still snipers shooting, so we put our steel helmets back on.

The people certainly looked well fed and well dressed. The streets were lined with green trees and modern buildings. All the stores were closed in holiday. Bicycles were so thick I have an idea there have been plenty accidents today, with tanks and jeeps overrunning the populace.

We entered Paris via Rue Aristide Briand and Rue d'Orleans[46]. We were slightly apprehensive, but decided it was all right to keep going as long as there were crowds. But finally, we were stymied by the people in the streets, and then above the din

---

46. *Therefore, from the south.*

we heard some not too-distant explosions - the Germans trying to destroy bridges across the Seine. And then the rattling of machine guns up the street, and that old battlefield whine of high-velocity shells just overhead. Some of us veterans ducked, but the Parisians just laughed and continued to carry on.

There came running over to our jeep a tall, thin, happy woman in a light brown dress, who spoke perfect American.

She was Mrs. Helen Cardon, who lived in Paris for 21 years and has not been home to America since 1935. Her husband is an officer in French Army headquarters and home now after two and a half years as a German prisoner. He was with her in civilian clothes.

Mrs. Cardon has a sister, Mrs. George Swikart, of 201 W. 72d St., New York, and I can say here to her relatives in America that she is well and happy. Incidentally, her two children Edgar and Peter, are the only two American children, she says, who have been in Paris throughout the entire war.

We entered Paris from due south and the Germans were still battling in the heart of the city along the Seine when we arrived, but they were doomed. There was a full French armored division in the city, plus American troops entering constantly.

The farthest we got in our first hour in Paris was near the Senate building, where some Germans were holed up and firing desperately. So, we took a hotel room nearby and decided to write while the others fought. By the time you read this, I'm sure Paris will once again be free for Frenchmen, and I'll be out all over town getting my bald head kissed. Of all the days of national joy I've ever witnessed this is the biggest.

8/29/44
Paris

The other correspondents have written so thoroughly and so well about the fantastic eruption of mass joy when Paris was liberated that I shall not dwell on it much longer.

But there are some little things I have to get out of my system, so we'll have at least this one more column on it.

Actually, the thing has floored most of us. I know that I have felt totally incapable of reporting it to you. It was so big I felt inadequate to touch it. I didn't know where to start or what to say. The words you put down about it sound feeble to the point of asininity.

I'm not alone in this feeling, for I've heard a dozen other correspondents say the same thing. A good many of us feel we have failed in properly presenting the loveliest, brightest story of our time. It could be that this is because we have been so unused, for so long, to anything bright.

At any rate, let's go back to the demonstration. From 2 o'clock in the afternoon until darkness around 10, we few Americans in Paris on that first day were kissed and hauled and mauled by friendly mobs until we hardly knew where we were.

Everybody kissed you - little children, old women, grown-up men, beautiful girls. They jumped and squealed and pushed in a literal frenzy.

They pinned bright little flags and badges all over you. Amateur cameramen took pictures. They tossed flowers and friendly tomatoes into your jeep. One little girl even threw a bottle of cider into ours.

As you drove along, gigantic masses of waving and screaming humanity clapped their hands as though applauding a fine performance in a theater. We in the jeeps smiled back until we had got grins on our faces. We waved until our arms gave out, and then we just waggled our fingers. We shook hands until our hands were bruised and scratched. If the jeep stopped, you were swamped instantly. Those who couldn't reach you threw kisses at you, and we threw kisses back.

They sang songs. They sang wonderful French songs we had never heard. And they sang 'Tipperary' and 'Madelon' and 'Over There' and the 'Marseillaise.'

French policemen saluted formally but smilingly as we passed. The French tanks that went in ahead of us pulled over to the sidewalks and were immediately swarmed over.

And then some weird cell in the mystic human makeup caused people to start wanting autographs. It began the first evening, and by the next day had grown to unbelievable proportions. Everybody wanted every soldier's autograph.

They shoved notebooks and papers at you to sign. It was just like Hollywood. One woman, on the second day, had a stack of neat little white slips, surely 300 of them, for people to sign.

That first afternoon only the main streets into the city were open and used, and they were packed with humanity. The side streets were roped off and deserted, because the Germans had feeble fortifications and some snipers there.

The weather was marvelous for liberation day, and for the next day too. For two days previously it had been gloomy and raining But on the big, day the sky was pure blue, the sun was bright and warm - a perfect day for a perfect occasion.

Paris seems to have all the beautiful girls we have always heard it had. The women have an art of getting themselves up fascinatingly. Their hair is done crazily, their clothes are worn imaginatively. They dress in riotous colors in this lovely warm season, and when the flag-draped holiday streets are packed with Parisians, the color makes everything else in the world seem gray.

As one soldier remarked, the biggest thrill in getting to Paris is to see people in bright summer clothes again.

Like any city, Paris has its quota of dirty and ugly people. But dirty and ugly people have emotions too, and Hank Gorrell got roundly kissed by one of the dirtiest and ugliest women I have ever seen. I must add that since he's a handsome creature he also got more than his share of embraces from the beautiful young things.

There was one funny little old woman, so short she couldn't reach up to kiss men in military vehicles, who appeared on the second day carrying a stepladder. Whenever a car stopped, she would climb her stepladder and let the boys have it with hugs, laughs and kisses.

The second day was a little different from the first. You could sense that during those first few hours of liberation, the people were almost animal-like in their panic of joy and relief and gratitude. They were actually crying as they kissed you and screamed, 'Thank you, oh thank you, for coming!'

But on the second day it was a deliberate holiday. It was a festival prepared for and gone into on purpose. You could tell that the women had prettied up especially. The old men had on their old medals, and the children were scrubbed and Sunday-dressed until they hurt.

And then everybody came downtown. By 2 in the afternoon the kissing and shouting and autographing and applauding were almost deafening. The pandemonium of a free and lovable Paris reigned again. It was wonderful to be here.

8/30/44
In Paris

As we drove toward Paris from the south, hundreds of Parisians - refugees and returning vacationists[47] - rode homeward on bicycles amidst the tanks and big guns.

Some Frenchmen have the facility for making all of us Nervous Nellies look ridiculous. There should be a nonchalant Frenchman in every war movie. He would be a sort of French Charlie Chaplin. You would have tense soldiers crouching in ditches and firing from behind low walls. And in the middle of it you would have this Frenchman, in faded blue overalls and beret and with a nearly burned-up cigaret in his mouth, come striding down the middle of the road past the soldiers.

I've seen that very thing happen about four times since D-Day, and you never can see it without laughing.

Well, the crowds were out in Paris like that while the shooting was still going on. People on bicycles would stop with one foot on the pavement to watch the firing that was going on right in that block.

As the French Second Armored Division rolled into the city at dangerous speed, I noticed one tank commander, with goggles, smoking a cigar, and another soldier in a truck playing a

---

47. *Vacationists in France in the summer of 1944? Ernie Pyle must have been mistaken...*

flute for his own amusement. There also were a good many pet dogs riding into the battle on top of tanks and trucks.

Amidst this fantastic Parisward battle traffic were people pushing baby carriages full of belongings, walking with suitcases, and riding bicycles so heavily loaded with gear that if they were to lay them down they had to have help to lift them upright.

And in the midst of it was a tandem bicycle ridden by a man and a beautiful woman, both in bright blue shorts, just as though they were holidaying - which undoubtedly they were.

You never saw so many bicycles in your life as in Paris. And they rig up the funniest contraptions on them, such as little two wheeled carts which they tow behind. And we saw a wagon rigged up so it could be pulled by two bicyclists riding side by side, like a team of horses.

For 24 hours, tanks were parked on the sidewalks all over downtown Paris. They were all manned by French soldiers, and each tank immediately became a sort of social center.

Kids were all over the tanks like flies. Women in white dresses climbed up to kiss men with grimy faces and, early the second morning, we saw a girl climbing sleepily out of a tank turret.

French soldiers of the armored division were all in American uniforms and they had American equipment. Consequently, most people at first thought we few Americans were French. Then, puzzled, they would say, 'English?' and we would say, 'No, American.' And then we would get a little scream and a couple more kisses.

Every place you stopped, somebody in the crowd would speak English. They apologized for not inviting us to their homes for a drink, saying they didn't have any. Time and again they would say, 'We've waited so long for you!' It almost got to be a refrain.

One elderly gentleman said that, although we were long in reaching France, we had come swiftly since then. He said the people hadn't expected us to be in Paris for six months after invasion day.

There are not many American soldiers in Paris. And it's unlikely there will be, at least for some time, because they are out over France going on with the war. Paris was not a military objective; its liberation so soon was more of a symbol. That's the reason the French Armored Division was assigned to the job.

The armies still fighting in the field were practically deserted for a few days by the correspondents, as we all wanted to get in on the liberation of Paris. There were so many correspondents, it got to be a joke, even among us. I think at least 200 must have entered the city that first day, both before and after the surrender.

The Army had picked out a hotel for us ahead of time, and it was taken over as soon as the city surrendered. But though it was a big hotel it was full before dark the first day so they have taken over another huge one across the street.

Hotel lift seems strange after so long in the field. My own room is a big corner one, with easy chairs, a soft bed, a bathroom and maid and hall-porter service. There is no electricity in the daytime, no hot water anytime, and no restaurant or bar, but outside of that the hotel is just about like peacetime.

Sitting here writing within safe walls, and looking out the window occasionally at the street thronged with happy people, it is already hard to believe there was a war; even harder to realize there still is a war.

8/31/44
Paris

Eating has been skimpy in Paris through the four years of German occupation, but reports that people were on the verge of starvation apparently were untrue.

The country people of Normandy all seemed so healthy and well fed that we said all along, 'Well, country people always face best, but just wait till we get to Paris. We'll see real suffering there.'

Of course, the people of Paris have suffered during these four years of darkness. But I don't believe they have suffered as much physically as we had thought.

Certainly, they don't look bedraggled and gaunt and pitiful, as the people of Italy did. In fact, they look to me just the way you would expect them to look in normal times. However, the last three weeks before the liberation really were rough. For the Germans, sensing that their withdrawal was inevitable, began taking everything for themselves. There is very little food in Paris right now. The restaurants either are closed or serve only the barest meals - coffee and sandwiches. And the 'national coffee', as they call it, is made from barley and is about the vilest stuff you ever tasted. France has had nothing else for four years.

If you were to take a poll on what the average Parisian most wants in the way of little things, you would probably find that he wants real coffee, soap, gasoline and cigarets.

***

Eating is the biggest problem right now for us correspondents. The Army hasn't yet set up a mess. We can't even get our rations cooked in our hotel kitchens, on account of the gas shortage.

So, we just eat cold K-rations and 10-in-1 rations in our rooms. For two days, most of us were so busy, we didn't eat at all and on the morning after the liberation of Paris, some of the correspondents were actually so weak from not eating that they could hardly navigate.

But the food situation should be relieved within a few days. The Army is bringing in 3,000 tons of food right away for the Parisians. That is only about two pounds per person, but it will help.

In little towns only ten miles from Paris, you can get eggs and wonderful dinners of meat and noodles. Food does exist, and now that transportation is open again, Paris should be eating soon.

***

Autos were almost nonexistent on the streets of Paris when we arrived. That first day, we met an English girl who had been here throughout the war, and we drove her for some distance in our jeep.

She was as excited as a child and said that was her first ride in a motorcar in four years. We told her that it wasn't a motorcar, that it was a jeep, but she said it was a motorcar to her.

Outside of war vehicles, a few French civilian cars were running when we arrived, but they were all in official use in the fighting. All of these had FFI (French Forces of the Interior) painted in rough white letters on the fenders, tops and sides.

***

Although it appears that the Germans did conduct themselves fairly properly up until the last few weeks, the French really detest them. One woman told me that, for the first three weeks of the occupation, the Germans were fine but that then they turned arrogant. The people of Paris simply tolerated them and nothing more.

The Germans did perpetrate medieval barbarities against leaders of the resistance movement as their plight became more and more desperate. But what I'm driving at is that the bulk of the population of Paris - the average guy who just gets along no matter who is here - didn't really fare too badly from day to day. It was just the things they heard about, and the fact of being under a bullheaded and arrogant thumb, that created the smoldering hatred for the Germans in the average Parisian's heart.

You can get an idea how they feel from a little incident that occurred the first night we were here.

We put up at a little family sort of hotel in Montparnasse. The landlady took us up to show us our rooms. A cute little French maid came along with her.

As we were looking around the room, the landlady opened a wardrobe door and, there on a shelf, lay a German soldier's cap that he had forgotten to take.

The landlady picked it up with the tips of her fingers, held it out at arm's length, made a face, and dropped it on a chair.

Whereupon the little maid reached up with her pretty foot and gave it a huge kick that sent it sailing across the room.

9/2/44
In France

We left Paris after a few days and went again with the armies in the field. In Paris, we had slept in beds and walked on carpeted floors for the first time in three months.

It was a beautiful experience, and yet for some perverse reason a great inner feeling of calm and relief came over us when we once again set up our cots in a tent, with apple trees for our draperies and only the green grass for a rug.

Hank Gorrell of the United Press was with me, and he said, 'This is ironic, that we should have to go back with the armies to get some peace.'

The gaiety and charm and big-cityness of Paris somehow had got a little on our nerves after so much of the opposite. I guess it indicates that all of us will have to make our return to normal life gradually and in small doses.

***

Paris unquestionably is a lovely city. It seems to me to have been but little hurt by the war. You can still buy almost anything imaginable if you have money. Everybody is well dressed. But prices are terrific, and already they have started zooming higher.

Those of us who expert to be coming home before long have made shopping tours and stocked up with gifts. And with the exception of perfume, which is dirt cheap, we pay about three times what we would at home for the same thing.

I'm sorry the restaurants couldn't open before we left. For, although I'm not much of a gourmet, I do value the sense of taste, and we've eaten enough meals in private homes and small-town restaurants over here to realize that it's all true about the French culinary genius.

They simply have a knack for making any old thing taste wonderful, just as the British have a knack for making everything taste horrible.

***

The other night we were talking about the beautiful women of Paris - as who doesn't?

One fellow said the women here were the most beautiful in the world.

But I said no, that wasn't true. You see women in America and England who are just as beautiful as any in Paris. But it seems that, here, the percentage of good-looking women is higher than in other

countries.

And another fellow said no, that wasn't it either. He thought the ratio was approximately the same in America and England and France. But, in Paris, a bigger percentage have the gift of getting themselves up to look devastating.

And I guess that's it.

***

We thought there were a lot of people on the streets those first two days. But you should have seen Paris a few days later, when the whole populace began to come out. By midafternoon it is almost impossible to drive in the streets because of the bicycles. They take up the entire street, as far as you can see. The sidewalks are packed. It's like Christmas shopping time at home.

Within three days, Paris was transformed from a city crackling and roaring with brief warfare into a city entirely at peace. Within three days, Paris was open for business as usual, and its attitude toward the war reminded me of Cairo after its threat of danger had gone.

***

As usual, those Americans most deserving of seeing Paris will be the last ones to see it, if they ever do. By that I mean the fighting soldiers.

Only one infantry regiment and one reconnaissance outfit of Americans actually came into Paris, and they passed on through the city quickly and went on with their war.

The first ones in the city to stay were such nonfighters as the psychological warfare and civil-affairs people, public-relations men and correspondents.

I heard more than one rear-echelon soldier say he felt a little ashamed to be getting all the grateful cheers and kisses for the liberation of Paris when the guys who broke the German army and opened the way for Paris to be free were still out there fighting without benefit of kisses or applause.

But that's the way things are in this world.

9/4/44
In France

The last time I was with the front-line medics - a battalion detachment in the Fourth Division - they showed me a piece in *The Stars and Stripes* about Congress passing the new $10-a-month pay increase for soldiers holding the combat infantrymen's badge[48].

This combat infantry badge is a proud thing, a mark of great distinction, a sign on a man's chest to show that he has been through the mill. The medical aidmen were feeling badly because the piece said they were not eligible for the badge.

Their captain asked me what I thought, and so did some of the enlisted aidmen. And I could tell them truthfully that my feelings agreed with theirs. They should have it. And I'm sure any combat infantryman would tell you the same thing.

Praise for the medics has been unanimous ever since this war started. And just as proof of what they go through, take this one detachment of battalion medics that I was with.

They were 31 men and two officers. And, in one seven-week period of combat in Normandy this summer, they lost nine men killed and ten wounded. A total of 19 out of 33 men - a casualty ratio of nearly 60 per cent in seven weeks!

As one aidman said, probably they have been excluded because they are technically noncombatants and don't carry arms. But he suggested that, if this was true, they could still be

---

48. The Combat Infantryman Badge is an American military decoration created in 1943 and awarded to U.S. Army soldiers, non-commissioned officers and officers of ranks under Colonel, having actively participated in combat in an infantry unit or in a special force after 6 December 1941.

given a badge with some distinctive medical marking on it, to set them off from medical aidmen who don't work right in the lines.

So, I would like to propose to Congress or the War Department or, whoever handles such things that the ruling be altered to include medical aidmen in battalion detachments and on forward.

They are the ones who work under fire. Medics attached to regiments and to hospitals further back do wonderful work too, of course, and are sometimes under shellfire. But they are seldom right out on the battlefield. So, I think it would be fair to include only the medics who work from battalion on forward.

I have an idea the original ruling was made merely through a misunderstanding, and that there would be no objection to correcting it.

***

You must hear about my new stove. You may remember that last winter in Italy we mentioned how practical and wonderful the little Coleman gasoline stove was for soldiers in the field[49]. Well, that remark had repercussions.

It seems the employees of the Coleman Stove Co., in Wichita Kas., were very pleased. It made them feel that they were doing something worthwhile for the war. So, in appreciation, they decided to make up a special stove as a gift for me.

---

49. Ernie Pyle had written that among the objects used by American soldiers on campaign, the Coleman portable camp stove was the most practical, after the Jeep. Coleman is the leading American brand of outdoor material, in particular for camping.

Ernie Pyle in Paris with his Coleman stove, made specifically for him by the workers at the Coleman factory. © *Photo Indiana State Museum*

We kept hearing about it over here for weeks and waited for it the way children wait for Christmas. The other correspondents were as excited about it as I was.

At last, it came. Boy, you should see it. It is an exact duplicate of the regular stove, except that this one is all handmade and chromium-plated and has my name engraved on it, like a loving cup.

One of the correspondents said, 'You can't light that, it's too pretty.' An Army colonel said, 'They should have sent a fireplace and a mantel along for you to exhibit it on.'

For days, there was a line of soldiers and correspondents at my tent wanting to see the stove. Twice we got ready to light it while photographers took pictures, but, at the last minute, we couldn't bear to, and put it away. The boys all kidded me and said they bet I never would light it.

Necessity finally drove me to it. That was in Paris. I had given my old stove to a friend, thinking I wouldn't need one anymore. But the eating situation in Paris was drastic at first, and we had only the rations we brought with us individually.

So, at last, I had to break down and light my stove in a hotel room in Paris. Some of the boys had joked and said it was so beautiful it probably wouldn't work. But it did. It practically melted the hotel walls down.

So, to all of you who had a hand in the stove, my thanks and gratitude. But if this keeps up, I'll have to be careful about admiring in print any Baldwin locomotives or steam-shovels.

9/5/44
Paris

This is the last of these columns from Europe. By the time you read this, the old man will be on his way back to America. After that will come a long, long rest. And after the rest - well, you never can tell.

Undoubtedly, this seems to you to be a funny time for a fellow to be quitting the war. It is a funny time. But I'm not leaving because of a whim, or even especially because I'm homesick.

I'm leaving for one reason only - because I have just got to stop. 'I've had it,' as they say in the Amy. I have had all I can take for a while.

I've been 29 months overseas since this war started: have written around 700,000 words about it; have totaled nearly a year in the frontlines.

I do hate terribly to leave right now, but I have given out. I've been immersed in it too long. My spirit is wobbly and my mind is confused. The hurt has finally become too great.

All of a sudden, it seemed to me that if I heard one more shot or saw one more dead man, I would go off my nut. And if I had to write one more column I'd collapse. So I'm on my way.

It may be that a few months of peace will restore some vim to my spirit, and I can go warhorsing off to the Pacific. We'll see what a little New Mexico sunshine does along that line,

Even after two and a half years of war writing there still is a lot I would like to tell. I wish right now that I could tell you about our gigantic and staggering supply system that keeps those great armies moving.

I'm sorry I haven't been able to get around to many branches of service that so often are neglected. I would like to have written about the Transportation Corps and the airport engineers and the wirestringers and the chemical mortars and the port battalions. To all of those that I have missed, my apologies But the Army over here is just too big to cover it all.

***

I know the first question everyone will ask when I get home is, 'When will the war be over?'

So, I'll answer even before you ask me and the answer is, 'I don't know.'

We all hope and most of us think it won't be too long now. And yet there's a possibility of it going on and on, even after we are deep in Germany. The Germans are desperate and their leaders have nothing to quit for.

Every day the war continues is another hideous blackmark against the German nation. They are beaten and yet they haven't quit. Every life lost from here on is a life lost to no purpose.

If Germany does deliberately drag this war on and on, she will so infuriate the world by her inhuman bullheadedness that she is apt to be committing national suicide.

In our other campaigns, we felt we were fighting, on the whole, a pretty good people. But we don't feel that way now. A change has occurred. On the Western Front, the Germans have shown their real cruelty of mind. We didn't used to hate them, but we do now.

The outstanding figure on this western front is Lieut. Gen. Omar Nelson Bradley. He is so modest and sincere that he probably will not get his proper credit, except in military textbooks. But he has proved himself a great general in every sense of the word. And as a human being, he is just as great. Having him in command has been a blessed good fortune for America.

***

I cannot help but feel bad about leaving. Even hating the whole business as much as I do, you come to be a part of it. And you leave some of yourself here when you depart. Being with the American soldier has been a rich experience.

To the thousands of them that I know personally and the other hundreds of thousands for who I have had the humble privilege of being a sort of mouthpiece, this then is to say goodbye - and good luck.

Ernie Pyle, in Montebourg, in Manche. © *Indiana State Museum 68.991.008.0233*

Contents

Introduction 5

A genuine miracle 9
The terrible waste of war 27
A great and narrow fringe of sadness 31
The lighter side of things 41
The European Campaign explained 45
A tour of the peninsula 49
When the Evangile of good-willed men thundered
through the skies 53
Hedgerow warfare 57

N.B.: We would like to thank the University of Indiana library (Lilly Library) which owns the Ernie Pyle typescripts.

Cover photo credit: © *Indiana State Museum 68.991.008.0279*

Zone tertiaire de Nonant - 14400 BAYEUX
Tel.: +33(0)2 31 51 81 31 - Fax: +33(0)2 31 51 81 32
E-mail: info@orepeditions.com - Website: www.orepeditions.com

Editor: Grégory Pique
Editorial coordination: Joëlle Meudic
Graphic design: Sophie Youf
English Translation: Heather Inglis

ISBN: 9782815106450 – © Éditions OREP 2022
Legal deposit: October 2020